Praise for *Chargin*

T0004193

"Who would have thought that Martin Luther, champion of the gospel of God's grace in Jesus Christ, would also be the prophetic voice of his time preaching vociferously against the idolatry of financial and market systems that exploit people and are destructive of the common good of society? What a gift for clergy and lay alike that Michael Grzonka has brought this 'forgotten Luther' to the table not only in his excellent translation of Luther's 'Exhortation to the Clergy to Preach against Exploitation,' but in his contextual preface and the insightful Foreword by Carter Lindberg. Wrestling with this material will be a joy for many and difficult for others, for within it you will find Luther himself challenging any complacency of discipleship and tepidness of witness within the cultural Christianity of our own time. In this study of Luther you will find grace informing social responsibility, faith active in love."

—Rev. Conrad A. Braaten, retired senior pastor,
Church of the Reformation, Washington, DC,
and co-initiator of The Forgotten Luther Project

"Usury seems like such an outdated concept, yet Grzonka's translation of this important (and oft-overlooked) treatise, coupled with his incisive commentary and thought-provoking questions for review and study, brings Luther's critique of greed firmly into the present day. As economic inequality continues to increase, Grzonka reminds readers that an economy based on inequality and exploitation is as reprehensible now as it was five hundred years ago. When practices and policies allow a small few to thrive and leave many fighting to survive, the church cannot remain silent. Luther's 'Exhortation' starkly challenges us to confront economic injustice with the conviction that exploitation is an affront to both conscience and faith. One can hope that this new translation and set of study resources gain as much attention as the original writing did five centuries ago. As Grzonka makes clear, its fierce call to action is needed now more than ever."

—Ryan P. Cumming, PhD, program director,
hunger education, ELCA World Hunger

"Brilliant! Bravo and thanks to Mick Grzonka for bringing to light such a profound 'Exhortation' from Luther, a powerful Christian blueprint for a fair economic order then, and certainly this very helpful and timely translation now. Grzonka makes this user-friendly for academy and congregation alike, with study notes, discussion questions, and more. I had the pleasure of getting acquainted with Mick at the Forgotten Luther III Conference we hosted at Saint Luke. Mick's enthusiasm for justice, faith, grace for all, and, yes, Luther is infectious. Looking forward to using *Charging Interest* in the congregation."

—Rev. Connie A. Miller, senior pastor, Saint Luke Lutheran Church, Silver Spring, Maryland

"Perhaps you've met Martin Luther the theologian or biblical scholar. In this wonderful work, Michael Grzonka introduces us to Martin Luther the economic critic. By contextualizing and translating Luther's fiery text 'Exhortation to the Clergy to Preach against Usury,' Grzonka gives us a Luther who connects, at root, just economic practices and Christian identity. Readers will benefit not only from Grzonka's faithful translation of Luther, but also from his helpful glossary of terms and thoughtful list of discussion questions for each section. I heartily recommend this book for those seeking wisdom on faithful Christian life in the midst of our economically unjust times."

—Rev. Dr. Justin Nickel, Frances and Baxter Weant Assistant Professor of Lutheran Studies, Lutheran Theological Southern Seminary of Lenoir-Rhyne University, and author of *The Work of Faith: Divine Grace and Human Agency in Martin Luther's Preaching*

"Many people think of Martin Luther as simply a 'spiritual' authority. Michael T. Grzonka dispels that notion. His sprightly translation and introduction of Luther's 'Exhortation to the Clergy to Preach against Exploitation' (1540) shows the reformer as a bold denouncer of public greed and a strong advocate of generosity toward the poor and unfortunate. In our own age of wretched excess, this is a welcome and bracing text."

—Rev. Dr. Mark D. Tranvik, professor of Reformation history and theology, Luther Seminary, St. Paul, Minnesota

"Charging interest might sound innocent, but take a closer look. Mick Grzonka introduces us to a little-known Luther whose outspoken critique of early capitalism has as much relevance for today as it did when it helped shape the political economies of post-Reformation Europe. As a Luther scholar, Carter Lindberg makes clear in his Foreword that this book is nothing less than an *exhortation* to pastors and lay leaders of the church today to confront the greed-based practices that have produced the economic disparity we see in the world today. Read at your own risk."

—Rev. Dr. Paul Wee, author of *The Forgotten Luther: Reclaiming the Social-Economic Dimension of the Reformation* (Fortress Press, 2016).

Charging Interest

Charging Interest

Medieval Wisdom for a
Modern Financial Crisis

Based on
Martin Luther's
"Exhortation to the Clergy to Preach
against Exploitative Interest" (1540)

Translation, Introduction, and Study Resources by
Michael T. Grzonka

Foreword by
Carter Lindberg

Fortress Press
Minneapolis

CHARGING INTEREST
Medieval Wisdom for a Modern Financial Crisis

Based on Martin Luther's "Exhortation to the Clergy to Preach against
Exploitative Interest" (1540)

Copyright © 2023 Fortress Press, an imprint of 1517 Media. All rights reserved.
Except for brief quotations in critical articles or reviews, no part of this book
may be reproduced in any manner without prior written permission from the
publisher. Email copyright@1517.media or write to Permissions, Fortress Press,
PO Box 1209, Minneapolis, MN 55440-1209.

All Scripture quotations, unless otherwise indicated, are from the New Revised
Standard Version Bible: Catholic Edition, copyright © 1989, 1993 National
Council of the Churches of Christ in the United States of America. Used by
permission. All rights reserved worldwide.

Scripture quotations marked (NRSV) are from the New Revised Standard Version
Bible, copyright © 1989 National Council of the Churches of Christ in the
United States of America. Used by permission. All rights reserved worldwide.

Scripture quotations marked (KJV) are from the King James Version.

Scripture quotations marked (NMB) are from the New Matthew Bible.
© 2016 by Ruth Magnusson (Davis). Published by Baruch House Publishing.

Cover image: An early Florentine banker or money changer. From Georgio
Chiarini's woodcut, 1490 (Florence, Italy). Smith Archive / Alamy Stock Photo
Cover design: Kristin Miller

Print ISBN: 978-1-5064-8846-2
eBook ISBN: 978-1-5064-8847-9

Contents

Abbreviations

BC   Luther, Martin. *The Book of Concord: The Confessions of the Evan-gelical Lutheran Church*. Edited by Robert Kolb and Timothy J. Wengert. Translated by Charles Arand, Eric Grittsch, Robert Kolb, William Russell, James Schaaf, Jane Strohl, and Timothy J. Wengert. Minneapolis: Fortress, 2000.

LW   Luther, Martin. *Luther's Works*. Edited by Helmut T. Lehmann, Jaroslav Pelikan, Christopher Boyd Brown, and Benjamin T. G. Mayes. American ed. 55 vols. St. Louis: Concordia; Philadelphia: Fortress, 1955–1986.

WA   Luther, Martin. *Luther's Werke: Kritische Gesamtausgabe. [Schriften.]*. 65 vols. Weimar: H. Böhlau, 1883–1993.

WATR Luther, Martin. *D. Martin Luthers Werke: Kritische Gesamtausgabe*. Edited by J. K. F. Knaake, G. Kawerau, et al. 58 vols. Weimar: H. Böhlau, 1883–.

Foreword

Kudos and many, many thanks to Mick Grzonka and Fortress Press for making accessible Luther's long-neglected pastoral-theological critique of laissez-faire capitalism. Luther's "Exhortation" that pastors expose and excommunicate unrepentant capitalist extortionists is both timely and shocking. It is timely in our present context of the extreme disparities in wealth and taxes, and it is shocking to those who think politics and economics should be kept out of the pulpit.

We forget or were not aware that Luther did not hesitate to call out people who conveniently ignored social justice while masquerading as upright. Throughout his ministry as pastor and theologian, Luther consistently confronted economic injustice with the gospel. He saw no contradictions in this stance because both the works-righteousness of medieval piety and the financial exploitation of the early modern economy were based on an ideology of achievement. The widespread medieval image of the ladder of virtues that facilitated success in attaining salvation was comparable to the corporate ladder that facilitated success in wealth and power. Both express the counterfeit gospel that a person's worth depends on achievement. The economic drive to acquire the world is the "other side of the coin" of salvation by works.

Unfortunately, few of Luther's many critiques of economic exploitation are easily accessible, since they are bound in various collections of Luther's writings mostly shelved in seminary and university libraries rather than churches. However, one fairly available source, often tucked away in the pastor's bookcase, is the Large Catechism, composed in 1529 for use in the church and included in *The Book of Concord* (BC). Here, beginning with his exposition of the first commandment, Luther directly confronts the mantra of his time and ours, so succinctly expressed by the actor Michael Douglas in the movie *Wall Street* when he proclaimed, "Greed is good" because it impels human progress. No, Luther thundered, greed is *not* good; greed is idolatry; greed breaks the greatest of all commandments: "You are to have no other gods." "There are some who think that they have God and everything they need when they have money and property; they trust in them and boast in them. . . . This is the most common idol on earth."[1]

Having clarified the issue, Luther listed examples of greed in his commentary on the seventh commandment. He directs his ire not at those he calls petty thieves but at the capitalists in the urban centers who willingly oppress the poor to amass more wealth for themselves: "We ought to be attacking the great, powerful archthieves with whom lords and princes consort . . . who daily plunder . . . all of Germany."[2] They "justify" their greed by the idolatry of the "laws" of the market and launder their reputations with philanthropy. The church's and pastors' responsibility is "to instruct and to reprove with God's Word"[3] all the economic activities that displace the common good by personal gain. The "public relations" problem for the pastor, of course, is that while exhortations to personal charity may be well received, criticism of the political economy that necessitates such charity steps on many ideological toes: "How skillfully Sir Greed can dress up to look like a pious man if that seems to be what the occasion requires, while he is actually a double scoundrel and a liar";[4] "God opposes usury and greed, yet no one realizes this because it is not simple murder and robbery. Rather usury is a more diverse, insatiable murder and robbery. Thus everyone should see to his worldly and spiritual office as commanded to punish the wicked and protect the pious."[5] Thus Luther exhorted preachers "to strip off the masks by which such rogues [usurers] adorn themselves as if they were righteous and pious."[6] Political and government leaders are then called on to restrain such revealed evils and promote the common good.[7]

Luther was under no illusions about reining in these economic and political actors, for after all, as he once noted, "a prince is a rare bird in

1 BC, 387.
2 BC, 417.
3 BC, 419.
4 LW 21:183; see also 44:107.
5 WA 51:422–23; see p. 103.
6 WA 51:332; see p. 23.
7 BC, 418–19.

heaven."[8] Nevertheless, the church is responsible to "speak the truth bold-ly"[9] "in the congregation."[10] The following "Exhortation to the Clergy to Preach against Exploitative Interest" vividly and forcefully exhibits Luther's lifelong commitment to explicate the gospel for social justice to the extent of preaching truth to power.

Carter Lindberg, Summer 2022

---

8 Use LW 21:345. See also Carter Lindberg, "Reclaiming Luther's Public Witness on Church, State, and War," in *The Forgotten Luther II: Reclaiming the Church's Public Witness*, ed. Ryan P. Cumming (Minneapolis: Fortress, 2019), 18–20.

9 LW 44:51.

10 LW 13:14–51.

Introduction

Compared with the abundance of publications about Martin Luther and the German Reformation he spawned, it is evident that contributions on the question of professional and economic ethics remain mostly footnotes. Articles taking on this subject from a Lutheran perspective are even fewer, especially those published in the English language.[1]

Martin Luther was no stranger to the influences that moneyed interests regularly apply to society. Often coercive in nature and purpose, medieval private wealth continually influenced the budding Reformation—from the Roman Catholic Church (arguably the largest corporation in Luther's Europe and its agricultural economy) to the big transnational trading houses and banks of the Fugger, Welser, Imhof, and Hochstätter families.

The modus operandi of the emerging money economy in Luther's time was what we today call "laissez-faire"—the market actors were free to do as they pleased with precious little oversight or regulation affecting their dealings. Given enough time, such willful disinterest from the authorities is known to favor the dominant players. Unsurprisingly, the medieval aristocracy, the Catholic Church, and the big trading houses thus frequently enjoyed the privilege of monopoly and cartel.

Large port cities such as Antwerp, at the mouth of the Rhine River in present-day Belgium, provided natural places to form "rings of merchants"—that is, cartels; Luther calls them *Gesellschaften*. Such groups coordinated prices and availability of goods across merchants, thereby anesthetizing or abolishing price formation under conditions of

---

1 Notable recent exceptions include two books developed to highlight Luther on economic matters: Carter Lindberg and Paul A. Wee, eds., *The Forgotten Luther: Reclaiming the Social-Economic Dimension of the Reformation* (Minneapolis: Lutheran University Press; Fortress, 2016); and Cumming, *Forgotten Luther II*.

truly free markets.[2] Active enforcement of competition by the authorities was a necessity yet to be recognized. Far from it, Luther frequently saw crown and commerce colluding in jointly establishing monopolies to maximize the profits of specific trading houses in return for favors rendered to those in power.[3]

Of the rulers Luther knew, Holy Roman emperor Charles V was especially vulnerable to blackmail by the Fugger banking house. In 1521, Jakob Fugger himself led a bank consortium of leading European banking houses in buying Charles's election. To secure Charles's emperorship over rival candidates, the group paid bribes of more than 113 million US dollars in today's money. This investment in medieval "campaign financing" paid off only two years later, when antimonopoly legislation was proposed at the Imperial Diet of 1523. To derail and bury the proposed legislation, Mr. Fugger only needed to "remind" Charles of this "favor"—such legislation was never again discussed.

LUTHER WROTE FREQUENTLY ON ECONOMIC TOPICS

Thus, it is not surprising that Luther wrote frequently on the temptations that emerged from the love of money. Although he often went to great lengths explaining the considerable inventiveness in methods for dishonestly separating people from their money, Luther was most concerned about the adverse consequences for ordinary people he observed all around him, including the hunger they experienced and their financial ruin.

In late 1519 and early 1520, he preached both a short and a long sermon on the topic of usury, elaborating on common but unfair commercial practices at the time. In 1524, he revisited the topic in his book *Trade and Usury.*[4] Again in 1529, in his Small and his Large Catechisms, Luther elaborated specifically on the understanding of unfair business

---

2 Roy Pascal, *Social Basis of the German Reformation: Martin Luther and His Times* (1933; repr., London: Watts, 1971), 181.

3 For example, early in its history, the Fugger firm held a near monopoly on the copper trade in Europe, courtesy of favorable arrangements with the Habsburg rulers in the late 1400s. Later, Charles V granted the Fugger firm exclusive rights to the mercury mines in Spanish Almaden as a security for credits extended to the crown by the Fugger bank.

4 Martin Luther, *Trade and Usury* [*Von Kauffshandlung und Wucher*]; LW 45:231–310; WA 15:279–322.

transactions as a form of stealing when explaining the seventh commandment. We often fail to view Luther's writings against the backdrop of an increasingly monetized economy whose description readily captures many modern characteristics:

> Formerly the nobles, if they had ready money, were wont to invest it in real estate, which gave employment to many persons and provided the country with necessities. The merchants employed capital of this kind in their regular trade, whereby they adjusted want and superfluity between the various countries, gave employment to many, and increased revenue of princes and states. Nowadays, on the other hand, a part of the nobles and merchants . . . employ all their available capital in dealing in money. Hence the soil remains untilled, trade in commodities is neglected, there is often increase of prices, the poor are fleeced by the rich, and finally even the rich go bankrupt.[5]

Since then, Luther's views have lost nothing of their sting and little of their relevance to the circumstances we live in today. During the Great Recession of 2007–9, interest rates fell close to zero, effectively making interest on a loan a minor concern. In 2021, rates were still there. At the same time, it became customary to routinely charge interest rates in excess of 20 percent per year on credit card debt and commercially provided student loans at rates close to and often in excess of 10 percent per year. Today we are in a position to grasp Luther's arguments more easily than we have been in two generations. Interested readers may find recent publications in the Further Reading at the end of this book. It includes references to Luther's perspective on a market economy and a book series called *The Forgotten Luther*, which explores the social dimension of his writings.

Despite all his earlier writing and preaching, the practice of taking excessively high interests on loans only grew during Luther's lifetime. At the height of a devastating price inflation that forced people to borrow

---

5 Lodovico Guicciardini (1521–89), nephew of medieval historian and statesman Francesco Guicciardini (1483–1540), as quoted in Richard Ehrenberg, *Capital and Finance in the Age of the Renaissance*, trans. H. M. Lucas (New York: Harcourt Brace, 1928), 243, https://archive.org/details/capitalandfinanc037633mbp/page/n1/mode/2up.

money just to buy their daily food, Luther returned to the subject of exploitative interest in his *Vermahnung an die Pfarrherrn gegen den Wucher zu predigen.*[6]

Aggravated by a drought and a mouse infestation, regional prices for basic food staples were driven up further by speculative buying and the hoarding of grain through aristocratic circles and by outsiders not living in the region. By 1539, bread became unavailable as hunger spread in Wittenberg, and people rioted in the market square.[7] In their desperate need to secure their "daily bread" and keep their farms operational, many required consumer credits, often on offer only under exploitative conditions. In short order, the excessive interest payments and other chicanery with their debt very predictably deprived many borrowers of their land, houses, and the very economic foundations of future livelihood.

In an attempt to mitigate the calamity, on April 7, 1539, Martin Luther wrote to the Wittenberg city council requesting the authorities provide food relief. That evening, Mayor Lucas Cranach visited Luther to explain that the shortage of grain was actively caused by foreign speculators keeping the grain away from markets. Thereupon, Luther wrote to the elector of Saxony two days later asking him to put a stop to noblemen who "so rashly thrive" from grain sold at elevated prices. Four days later, Luther followed up his letter with a "very hard, pointed sermon" in which he called godless "the avarice of usurers" and called the usurers themselves "robbers and murderers."[8] His reference to this price inflation caused by nobles and peasants supports[9] that Luther likely began with the "Exhortation" soon thereafter. His original handwritten manuscript survives in full (see figure 1).

Sin of Usury Not Limited to Monetary Interest

According to Luther, when viewed theologically, the taking of exploitative, excessive interest, in its various manifestations, is an outflow of sin. But

---

6   The historic circumstance and detail leading up to the writing of Luther's sermon are reported in the introduction to the German version of this writing, which appears in WA 51:331–424. The introduction begins on p. 325; see also Martin Luther, *Luther's Works* 61:275–328 (St. Louis: Concordia, 2021).

7   Edith Eschenhagen, "Beiträge zur Sozial- und Wirtschaftsgeschichte der Stadt Wittenberg in der Reformationszeit," *Lutherjahrbuch* 9 (1927; repr., 1967): 86–87.

8   See Martin Luther, "Table Talk," LW 54:251–364, # 4496; WATR 4:345, # 4496.

9   See p. 102.

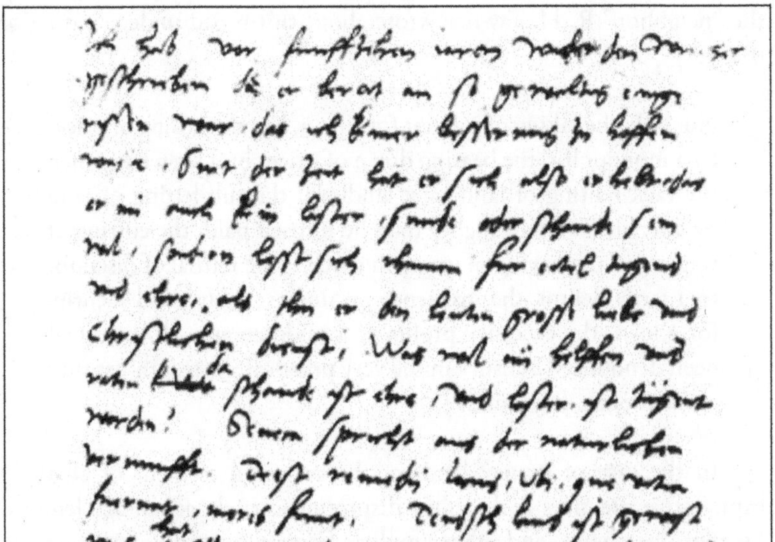

Figure 1: The first page of the manuscript of the 1540 "Exhortation," written in Luther's own hand. *Source:* https://digital.slub-dresden.de/werkansicht/dlf/156496/199.

for Luther, usury included not only the practice of loaning money under conditions that testify to a lender's willful acceptance, if not outright intent, of damaging the borrower. In that same sense, usury, for Luther, included any economic behaviors that originate from egoistical and personal enrichment and that, in their aggregate, serve to inflict damage on the "neighbor." R. H. Tawney wrote about this broad understanding of usury:[10]

> Not only the taking of interest for a loan, but the raising of prices by a monopolist, the beating down of prices by a keen bargainer, the rack-renting of land by a landlord, the sub-letting of land by a tenant at a rent higher than he himself paid, the cutting of wages and the paying of wages in truck,[11] the refusal of discount to a tardy debtor, the insistence on unreasonably good security for a loan, the excessive profits of a middleman—all these had been denounced as usury in the very practical thirteenth-century manual of St. Raymond.[12]

In the case of money lending, the common element of all these exploitative practices is that they disproportionately advantage lenders. Lenders, merchants, and other suppliers frequently used unfair commercial practices as tools to permanently seize the fruits of their neighbor's labor. In this way, they actively caused them calamity, need, and poverty and, in the ultimate consequence, destroyed their economic basis by obtaining their lands and property.

DRACONIAN MEASURES AGAINST UNREPENTANT USURERS

Luther resolved to call on the pastors to publicly denounce the activities of those avaricious lenders—the usurers. He pointed out that such businessmen live unmolested among Christians in their congregations and neighborhoods, allowing them to go on pretending that there is nothing wrong with their business practices. Luther pointedly disagreed: many such lenders fancy themselves to be in God's place—a blatant offense against the first commandment. Luther wrote, "Not only is Mammon

---

10 R. H. Tawney, *Religion and the Rise of Capitalism* (New York: Penguin, 1937), 131, https://ia801600.us.archive.org/31/items/in.ernet.dli.2015.275610/2015.275610.Religion-And.pdf.

11 Paying "in truck" refers to paying in kind, not in money.

12 Saint Raymond of Penyaford (1185–1275) was a Spanish Dominican friar who compiled the Decretals of Gregory IX, a collection of canonical laws that remained a major part of church law until the 1917 Code of Canon Law abrogated it.

their god, but through their Mammon, they themselves now want to be god to the world and fancy to be worshipped accordingly."[13]

Luther calls on the clergy to implement immediate and drastic consequences for such blasphemous behavior: unrepentant usurers should be excommunicated until such a time that they repent. He instructed pastors to refuse these usurers absolution, reject their participation in Holy Communion, and even deny their Christian burials.

A CONSIDERATE APPROACH TO INTEREST RATES

As in his earlier writings, Luther does not generally reject all lending as exploitative or usurious. Rather, he continues to request carefully crafted exemptions on behalf of needy individuals who must rely on interest payments as their exclusive source of income—widows, orphans, the sick, and those no longer able to work—provided the interest rate does not exceed some 5 percent.

Only in passing does Luther mention the concept of *Zinskauf*,[14] since he had extensively covered it in his earlier *Treatise on Usury*[15] and his *Trade and Usury*. In a fair *Zinskauf*, the collection by the lender varies with the actual future yield of crops grown on a piece of land sold by the debtor to obtain cash now. Thus, far from condemning the emerging money economy in an all-out way, Luther had this construction of *Zinskauf* in mind to literally make the lender "take an interest" in the future affairs of the borrower; that is, the risk is shared by both parties. Against this backdrop, Luther's text considers interest rates of 4 to 6 percent justifiable.

---

13 See p. 75.

14 "[*Zinskauf* was a] financial transaction, for which no direct equivalent exists in modern finance[; it] essentially was a contract in which the rights to use a piece of land or other property were sold in exchange for fixed payments over a specified period of time. To avoid the appearance of usury, the creditor in this transaction was regarded as the buyer who purchased a fixed income from the debtor, who then merely was considered to be the seller of a predetermined stipend." David W. Jones, *Reforming the Morality of Usury: A Study of Differences That Separated the Protestant Reformers* (Dallas: University Press of America, 2004), 53. For more on *Zinskauf*, see p. 17.

15 Martin Luther, *On Usury* [*Sermon vom Wucher*], WA 6:31–60. Reprinted as part of the later *Trade and Usury*. See footnote 4, p. 2.

WHY WOULD 5 PERCENT INTEREST SEEM ACCEPTABLE?

Monetary policy, as we recognize it today, was not a tool available at the time. There was no central bank controlling the money supply. At the same time, the biblical prohibition against taking any interest at all is still the official policy of the Catholic Church, though it is widely ignored. Interest rates on loans can be whatever the market can bear. In a calamity such as a bad harvest, interest rates could quickly jump to 20, 30, or even 40 percent.[16] Why would Luther propose a rate of 5 percent annual interest as acceptable?

A comprehensive reason was recently confirmed by French economist Thomas Piketty analyzing "Capital in the 21st Century." According to Piketty's research, the return on (arable) land has been very constant at just about that rate over long periods of time:

> For the sake of concreteness, let us note . . . that the average rate of return on land in rural societies is typically on order of 4–5 percent. In the novels of Jane Austen and Honoré de Balzac the fact that land (like government bonds) yields roughly 5 percent of the amount of capital invested . . . is so taken for granted that it often goes unmentioned. Contemporary readers were well aware that it took capital on the order of 1 million francs to produce an annual rent of 50,000 francs. For nineteenth-century novelists and their readers the relation between capital and annual rent was self-evident and the two measuring scales were used interchangeably as if rent and capital were synonymous or perfect equivalents in two different languages.[17]

Likewise, in Luther's agricultural economy, it would have been common knowledge—too insignificant to even warrant mention—that one could produce some 5 percent of profit from agricultural resources and labor. Those 75–90 percent of the population still working the lands as peasants or serfs could never hope to produce the outsized returns routinely expected of a trading and finance economy. Luther therefore recognized rates beyond what was economically feasible for the borrower

---

16 See p. 52.
17 Thomas Piketty, *Capital in the Twenty-First Century* (Cambridge, MA: Belknap Press of Harvard University Press, 2014), 52–53.

as unsustainable. In the long run, such excessive rates damage, erode, and ultimately annihilate the economic foundations of borrowers such as peasants, craftsmen, and the common burghers.

Quite foreseeably, debtors locked into debt at exploitative interest rates would, sooner rather than later, find themselves unable to come up with even the interest, let alone pay back the principal. Luther very colorfully describes such borrowers as "eaten" by lenders insisting on their interest payments, regardless of debtors' ability to pay them:

> 78. Therefore, whoever lends out one hundred gulden at Leipzig now takes 40 percent annual interest—that is, he devours a peasant or citizen in one year. If he lends out a thousand gulden, he takes four hundred gulden each year in interest—that is, he devours a knight or rich nobleman in one year. If he lends out ten thousand, he takes four thousand gulden a year in interest—that is, he eats a rich squire in a year.[18]

These considerations demonstrate that we need to reflect on the "Exhortation" of 1540 in the context of its time. Martin Luther was no stranger to the economic thinking of his day. His father rose as a successful entrepreneur in the local mining industry. As an Augustinian vicar in 1515, Luther was responsible for eleven cloisters in Thuringia and Meissen at a time when cloisters were often among the largest economic entities of the medieval agricultural economy. In his early treatises on usury, Luther explains in great detail the countless tricks and techniques used by contemporary tradesmen to cheat in their daily dealings. However, attempting to claim Martin Luther as "Germany's first political economist"[19] is as ill conceived as would be an outright dismissal of his text for its failure to distinguish between investment loans (that create new products) and consumer credits abused to pay for the necessities of life. Luther's time, with the likely exception of the headquarters of the big banking houses, only knew of consumer credits.

---

18 See p. 52.
19 Gunter Fabiunke, *Martin Luther Als Nationalökonom* (Berlin: Akademie-Verlag, 1963); and Karl Marx, *Capital: A Critique of Political Economy* (Chicago: Charles H. Kerr, 1909). Karl Marx, whose paternal line supplied rabbis to the German town of Trier since 1723, quotes extensively from Luther's "Exhortation" and other publications of Luther in volumes 1 and 3.

INSISTING ON A PASTORAL VIEW OF THE ECONOMY

Luther's 1540 "Exhortation" is significant for a number of reasons. What Luther's view on economic topics continues to bring to the conversation, both then and perhaps even more so today, is his insistence that questions about the economic behavior of believers and the adequacy of the economic framework in which they are required to act must be viewed from the angle of "love of neighbor."

His pastoral view on economy strikes us moderns as utterly naïve and out of touch with our experience of present-day reality. But arguably, this is precisely the ingredient missing from our own conversation when we consider contemporary economies. It is the eye trained on the needs of the neighbor that can liberate our public discourse from being stuck in angrily enumerating the failures of the current economy and its leaders. It is this gaze at the supposed benefactors of economic activity that easily redirects and advances our conversation to a process of reimagining how to *transform our economy into what it once was and still ought to be*—a tool to serve human beings with all their needs and wants. By contrast, today's "finance-dominated capitalism"[20] has severed itself completely from serving the existential needs of humans. It evolved to generate profits from new mechanisms no longer tied to the production of goods or services for human consumption and is instead solely serving the monetary and business needs of other financial entities. It is this detachment that Luther senses when he observes the usury around him has become a self-serving practice, and the usurers applying it have switched allegiance to a different god, now worshipping the god of Mammon. In the process, they willfully accept damaging their fellow human beings, as Luther recognized some five hundred years ago: "A usurer does not care if the entire world dies of hunger—if only he can have his profit."[21]

Perhaps most important today is that Luther's pastoral view recognizes human economic actors in their perpetual, sinful vulnerability to the love of money, to temptation, greed, and selfish behavior. Most of us are far from acting like the ruthlessly selfish but generally act as rational *Homo economicus* populating contemporary economic models. Still, most of us continue to be sinful and flawed human beings—in our roles as

---

20 Kathryn Tanner, *Christianity and the New Spirit of Capitalism* (New Haven, CT: Yale University Press, 2019), 11–25.

21 See paragraph 204, p. 95.

lenders as well as borrowers. Like our medieval forbearers, we often fail
to do the right thing when engaging in economic action: we were then,
still are, and will remain the very same sinful beings that Luther writes
about in this tract.

THREE THOUGHTS TO CONSIDER

I would offer three reasons why Luther's text warrants our attention today,
especially at a time where economic uncertainty is back on the personal
agenda of believers and nonbelievers alike.[22]

Economic Reality Includes Man-Made Calamity

The "Exhortation" testifies that Luther clearly knew to distinguish between
adversities that "just happen" and calamities deliberately created by men
exploiting their fellow men. For example, bad harvests are caused by missing or ill-timed rain or by too much of it. This is simply a reality beyond
human control. Human solidarity, creative cooperation, and compassion
for others help us mitigate the fallout from such catastrophes and increase
common preparedness should they occur again. Because such disasters
cannot be prevented, we rely on one another—with the help of God—to
relieve their consequences.

Beyond that, however, Luther also observed firsthand a very different kind of disaster that was wholly man-made. Living and preaching
in Wittenberg, a town of some 2,200 inhabitants, he witnessed the consequences of a food shortage. In Luther's view, rather than being miti-
gated through solidarity among the people, the situation was aggravated
into an all-out famine by the actions of a few individuals who recognized
an opportunity for outsized profit.[23] The sheer need to buy something

---

22 A Federal Reserve survey finds that in 2018, almost 40 percent of American adults
   would need to "finance"—that is, borrow—to cover a surprise $400 emergency
   need. Board of Governors of the Federal Reserve System, *Report on the Economic
   Well-Being of U.S. Households in 2018*, May 2019, https://www.federalreserve.gov/
   publications/files/2018-report-economic-well-being-us-households-201905.pdf.
23 Luther's small-town view, as captured in this "Exhortation," has been challenged.
   Eschenhagen suggests a larger context of sizable inflation is also to blame: Saxony
   imported inflation from a general oversupply of precious metals. See Eschenhagen, "Beiträge," 79–84. The excess in precious metals is occasionally attributed to
   perpetual influx from Spanish possessions in the new world.

(anything) to eat drove people to take on loans at excessive and ultimately ruinous interest rates. What is more, these loans were often provided by the very individuals whose business activities had created food shortages and sky-high prices in the first place. In his "Exhortation," we learn that Luther clearly differentiates between the consequences of unpreventable disasters and those of calamities caused solely by the choices of some lenders seeking their own profits and advantages.

Taking an interest rate on a loan that is known to be unsustainable by the borrower—that is, whose bankruptcy is willfully accepted by the lender—is solely the choice of that lender. Lenders could choose otherwise, but they decide not to. Therefore, those deciding to demand such exploitative interest, not by God's choice but by their very own decision, make themselves into usurers. For Luther, their behavior is indistinguishable from that of devils at work: "Looking at such conduct with our evangelical hearts, we must conclude that it is not people but indeed hordes of veritable devils that rampage around in human masks."[24]

No Economic System Is Ordained by God

From this first insight follows a corollary: that people can choose how they behave in economic transactions. Whatever they decide, though, they personally own the consequences of their choice. Furthermore, individuals' economic choices are embedded in the economic framework their society has elected. Luther therefore also calls on the rulers—politicians in today's parlance—to do their job to design and enforce an economic framework to conduct business and reign in the evildoers.

Rulers do thus also have a choice to make. Whether they respond to their duty actively or through chosen inaction, Luther recognizes the resulting economic framework as under the shaping power of humankind. Economic order is, therefore, created by people and not a God-ordained nor a God-endorsed state of affairs. Although many continue suggesting it, in economics, the proverbial "invisible hand" of Adam Smith is precisely *not* the hand of God. Smith himself, the moral philosopher who lived some two hundred years after Luther, did not believe this[25]—and neither would have Martin Luther, as his "Exhortation" confirms. It

---

24 See p. 94.

25 Jesse Norman, *Adam Smith: What He Thought, and Why It Matters* (London: Allen Lane, 2018).

follows that any current economic order is what the people—and especially their government—make it to be. It follows further that economic rules can and must be changed when better concepts emerge or when the recognition of gross injustices demands reconsideration. In Luther's view of the Two Kingdoms, the responsibility to erect and enforce a just and productive economic order rests with the government of the worldly kingdom—the ruling princes of Luther's time and our politicians today.

Protestantism Needs to Confront the Topic of a Just Economy

The third and perhaps most significant insight is that Luther requires the church—namely, through the voices of its clergy—to preach publicly on the issue of just economics. The economy affects all church members who are *in* this world. And as expressed anew in Luther's writings, Christianity has clear expectations of what a just economy looks like. The church has a duty not to "fix" the economy but to perpetually hold up a yardstick of just economics against whatever current system is deemed acceptable by its creators, peddlers, and benefactors. As the Barmen Theological Declaration, passed at the birth hour of the Confessing Church in 1934 Nazi Germany, phrases it, "We reject the false doctrine that there could be areas of our life in which we would not belong to Jesus Christ but to other lords, areas in which we would not need justification and sanctification through him."[26]

This contrasts with a long-standing tradition within much of contemporary Protestantism that asserts the economy to be a place that is acting under a set of self-ordained and self-contained rules that cannot and must not be examined in the harsh light of the Christian gospel. Many churches render commendable social services to mitigate the social fallout from our current economic order—be it homelessness, food insecurity, or other poverty in the midst of material abundance. But never once do they ask why the conditions of their brothers and sisters in the lowest areas of society refuse to improve. Observing the flagrant inconsistencies originating from this ecclesiastical cocoon of self-limitation, Catholic archbishop Hélder Câmara once observed, "When I give food

---

26 Quoted in Robert McAfee Brown, *Kairos: Three Prophetic Challenges to the Church* (Grand Rapids, MI: Eerdmans, 1990), 157.

to the poor, they call me a saint. When I ask why they are poor, they call me a communist."[27]

Therefore, when Pope Francis calls rampant capitalism "a new tyranny," asserting that "such an economy kills,"[28] he exemplifies what Luther was saying in 1540: there are simply no grounds for flatly excluding the topic of proper economic behavior and a just economy from the church's preaching. Many mature Christians crave to consciously apply their faith also to the difficult topics of work life and economy and especially to money, credit, and interest. To that end, Luther's "Exhortation" certainly supplies a genuine starting point for an overdue conversation on what a truly just economy could look like and how to implement it.

RECEPTION OF THE TRACT

Luther's "Exhortation to Preach against Exploitative Interest" is one of his more successful writings. Josef Klug printed and put it on the market on Christmas in 1539. We know this from a letter written by Philip Melanchthon, dated December 23, 1539, which contained a copy of the new book. Thanks to popular demand, Klug produced two additional print runs in 1540. Johann Petreius in Nuremberg reprinted them for sale in the southern parts of Germany, the area that included the headquarters of the large monopoly firms Luther continued to criticize. A translation into Latin in 1554 provided an international edition that was readily understood across all of Europe.

A FEW WORDS ON FORMATTING AND TRANSLATION

For improved readability and unless otherwise noted, Luther's verbatim quotes of Bible passages in the original text were replaced by the corresponding text from the New Revised Standard Version, Catholic Edition.

---

27 Dom Hélder Câmara was Roman Catholic Archbishop of Olinda and Recife, Northeastern Brazil; quoted here from *Encyclopaedia Britannica*, s.v. "Hélder Pessoa Câmara," last modified February 3, 2022, https://www.britannica.com/biography/Helder-Pessoa-Camara.

28 Pope Francis, *Evangelii Gaudium: Apostolic Exhortation on the Proclamation of the Gospel in Today's World*, Vatican, November 24, 2013, http://w2.vatican.va/content/francesco/en/apost_exhortations/documents/papa-francesco_esortazione-ap_20131124_evangelii-gaudium.html.

In his essay, Luther refers to the Old Testament "book of Sirach." Although Luther quotes from it liberally, today, Sirach is in neither the Protestant nor Jewish canon. Abbreviated "Sir," the book continues to be used in the Catholic and Orthodox traditions and is readily available in corresponding editions of the Bible. Lutherans count Sirach among a group of books called Deuterocanonical.

I have divided Luther's text into parts (part I, II, etc.). These parts, their titles, and the added paragraph numbering are not in Luther's original text. They are added here to increase readability and to aid references and quotes.

Luther uses the currency of German *florin*, which also translates to "gulden." For improved readability, we use the word *gulden* throughout. This affects neither Luther's argument nor his math.

The German used in Luther's essay is as far from modern German as American English is from the English of William Tyndale.[29] The translation presented here aims to preserve Luther's crisp, direct, and straightforward writing style. Luther preferred simple words and short sentences; however, many thoughts are carried across a semicolon (like we just did), sometimes repeatedly in one sentence. This can make for very long constructs that many modern readers find difficult. When translating, we followed the idea that in Luther's times, those able to read would have read aloud the essay to their neighbors and friends. When such readers paused at colons or semicolons, listeners would usually not be able to distinguish this pause from that at the end of a full sentence. It therefore seemed permissible to make a conscious effort to break down the most complex sentences into separate ones for increased readability.

TRANSLATING *USURY* AS "EXPLOITATIVE INTEREST"

Usury as a word has fallen into disuse in a time when we expect to pay interest for every loan taken and to receive interest payments on monies loaned, for example, as certificates of deposits.

---

29 Luther's original German is difficult even for modern German speakers and does not readily lend itself to translation. As an illustration, consider the example of Cor 13:4–5 as written by William Tyndale: "Love suffreth longe and is corteous. Love envieth not. Love doth not frowardly swelleth not, dealeth not dishonestly, seketh not her awne, is not provoked to anger, thynketh not evyll." Although still perfectly understandable, it often takes considerable effort to fully examine the precise meaning of each word and phrase.

Luther witnessed the meaning of *usury* evolve over his lifetime. The Catholic Canon Law continued to prohibit the taking of any interest at all, viewing it as unbiblical. At the same time, the Catholic Church and general commerce widely used methods to get around this prohibition, and taking interest in money lending became accepted practice. What, then, distinguishes "usury" from mere "interest" in today's sense?

The key distinction for Luther is that usury expects payments at interest rates so high—up to 40 percent annually—that the lender predictably and willfully accepts the long-term economic bondage and indeed the likely economic ruin of the borrower. Credit granted under usurious conditions is, therefore, deliberately exploitative of the borrower and is typically accepted only by those coerced into borrowing at the mercy of some lender of last resort.

Lenders become usurers when they willfully demand interest rates that bring damage and bodily harm to the borrower. The term *exploitative interest* seems to capture this meaning adequately.

DEROGATORY TERMS USED BY LUTHER

As was common practice at the time, Luther hurls a plethora of creative and colorful but derogatory terms at those with whom he disagreed. Many of these terms were readily understood by his contemporaries, but they have no adequate translation in modern English. Because these words shed light on the color of Luther's language, some of them are explained here—not least to add to a reader's delight.

Geizwanst

A typical German-language construction is combining two words to give the combination a new meaning. Here, the word for "stinginess" (*Geiz*) is combined with the word for "paunch" or "belly" (*Wanst*). Put together in *Geizwanst*, they form a derogatory term for a miser whose stinginess against others has fattened him to the point of sporting a veritable potbelly. It is translated here as *miser-belly*.

Stuhlräuber

Stuhlräuber describes a person who, without ever getting out of their chair, commits the most atrocious of crimes. A connotation is that the

Stuhlräuber does so through seemingly legitimate actions. Commonly translated as swivel-chair robber or armchair bandit, other contemporary translations could also be *desktop bandit* or *cubicle criminal.*

Scharrhans (Plural, Scharrhansen)

Scharrhans is a derogatory term for a clumsy peasant. It is here translated as *clodhopper,* an English term introduced to describe people "hopping around" in crude, heavy-duty shoes often made of wood.

COMMERCIAL CONCEPTS MENTIONED IN THE TEXT

Luther's text references and elaborates on commercial concepts in economic use in his time. The most important ones are explained here.

Fürkauf

Fürkauf is a practice where middlemen front-run and corner the market to buy up the supply of a (scarce) good, only to resell it themselves at higher prices. In medieval times, this was often done quite openly by traders who would buy from farmers on their way to the downtown marketplaces. Just outside the city gates, the traders would buy up all of the farmers' goods before themselves offering these same goods on the same markets in short order—at higher prices. Evidently, such a practice has no added value or benefit to consumers.

In the case at hand, *Fürkauf* was performed in Luther's Saxony to help corner the local market for food that was already in scarce supply. This practice aggravated a shortage of food into a famine for those consumers who could no longer afford food at the resulting elevated prices.

Zinskauf

Based on the definition provided in note 14 (p. 7) and repeated below in note 30,[30] *Zinskauf* is thus some form of purchasable rent. Martin Luther

---

30 "[*Zinskauf* was a] financial transaction, for which no direct equivalent exists in modern finance[; it] essentially was a contract in which the rights to use a piece of land or other property were sold in exchange for fixed payments over a specified period of time. To avoid the appearance of usury, the creditor in this transaction

made it a subject of his *Treatise on Usury* and his *Trade and Usury*, criticizing clergy of the Catholic Church for violating the spirit, albeit not the letter, of anti-usury laws. The Catholic Church tolerated *Zinskauf* as a way to avoid prohibitions on usury. Since *Zinskauf* was an exchange of a fixed amount of money for annual income, it was considered a sale rather than a loan. But abuses were common and committed with impunity.[31] Luther would consider most abuses usurious because they usually favored lenders. To make *Zinskauf* a fair transaction, Luther required that a specific piece of land be identified for a given deal and the borrower's payments be tied to the actual crop yield of this very land. In contrast to a fixed interest rate, this means that in bad years, the debtor's payment would be reduced in lockstep with his economic ability to produce the payments, while in good years, payments would be nominal, supported by sufficient harvests. Luther repeats this condition in the "Exhortation" (see paragraph 222, p. 103).

Zinskauf, when done fairly, can be a reasonable construction with variable yield suited for the vagaries of an economy based on agricultural value creation. Done Luther's way, a *Zinskauf* is not unlike us moderns owning common shares of a dividend-paying firm. Like with proper *Zinskauf*, the dividend flow is tied to a specific company and will vary with that firm's business fortunes.

Schadewacht

Schadewacht is a concept much like modern-day mortgage insurance. When their own stake in a recently purchased house is deemed too low, would-be homeowners are often required to sign and pay for extra insurance to benefit the lender. That insurance protects lenders from damages in a situation where borrowers just walk away from a property that is diminished in value through disrepair, neglect, or damage caused through no fault of the lender. Should borrowers just walk away from such damaged property or simply default on their payment without such insurance, lenders stand to suffer losses through no fault of their own.

---

was regarded as the buyer who purchased a fixed income from the debtor, who then merely was considered to be the seller of a predetermined stipend." Jones, *Morality of Usury*, 53.

31 For a list of common variants, see Hans J. Prien, *Luthers Wirtschaftsethik* (Göttingen: Vandenhoeck & Ruprecht, 1998), 62–63.

In this spirit, *Schadewacht*—literally, "my loss stays awake"—was an add-on payment made by the borrower, together with regular payments of interest and payback of principal. The idea was to accrue a buffer in case borrowers defaulted on their loan. However, as Luther explains, the payments made as *Schadewacht* were kept by the lender even if no default ever occurred, amounting to a net increase of the lender's profits.

REVIEW QUESTIONS

The paragraphs of each part are followed by a series of Review Questions designed to guide a review of Luther's text and focus the reader's attention on important insights within the original work. These questions are meant to support text comprehension and emphasize key passages of Luther's text.

STUDY QUESTIONS

Study Questions support the application of Luther's thinking to daily practice and the society we live in today. These questions aim to foster discussions among the participants by helping the group reflect on the meaning of Luther's words as they may apply to today's realities.

LEADER NOTES

A section designed to aid group leaders can be found at the end of the book. It provides answers and helpful hints to some but not all of the Review and Study Questions.

ACKNOWLEDGMENT

I would like to thank Carter Lindberg for his continued support and encouragement.

* * *

EXHORTATION TO THE CLERGY TO PREACH AGAINST EXPLOITATIVE INTEREST

Martin Luther

Part I

Raising Voices against the Shame of Usury

1. I wrote against usury fifteen years ago, when it was already so rampant that I had no hope for any recovery. Since then, usury has escalated to the point that it no longer wants to be vice, sin, or shame but praises itself for proper virtue and honor, as if it would show people great love and as if it were providing some Christian service. What will help now that shame has become honor and vice turned virtue? From the view of natural reason, Seneca says, "There is no remedy where what has been considered a vice becomes a habit."[1] Germany is no longer what it ought to be: tiresome avarice and the taking of exploitative interest have destroyed it.

2. But for God's sake, I beseech all preachers and pastors that they neither keep quiet nor cease preaching against such usury and continue cautioning and warning the people. Although we cannot curtail usury—for that has now become all but impossible, not only for our preaching, but also for the entire secular government—our exhortation hopes to rescue at least a few from such Sodom and Gomorrah [Gen 19:14]. But although we have to leave a lot of good friends to perish in it because of their willfulness—as it was with Lot—we ourselves refuse to stop here. Nor shall our silence make us partake in their sin and punishment.

Instead, we raise our voice—as far as we are able to—and declare that usury is not a virtue but indeed great sin and shame. During the course of this year, therefore, let anyone obliged by his conscience and ministry be swayed to teach and warn his parishioners to beware of usury and

---

1 Latin: *Deest remedii locus, ubique vitia fuerunt, mores fiunt.*

avarice and to strip off the masks by which such rogues [usurers] adorn themselves as if they were righteous and pious.

DIFFERENCE BETWEEN LENDING AND USURY

3. In short and emphasizing the essential and most important, one should state unmistakably and clearly to the people that *where one lends money and demands or takes more or better money in return, that is usury—as damned by all laws.* That is why all those are usurers who take 5, 6 percent or more of the borrowed money and should behave accordingly. We call them idolatrous servants of Mammon or stinginess that cannot be saved unless they repent [Matt 6:24]. Likewise, it should be said that when lending grain, barley, and other goods, it is usury—that is, to steal and rob—if more or better goods are demanded in return.

4. For lending means giving someone my money, goods, or equipment so that he can use them as long as he needs them, or as long as I can and will let him have them, and then return them to me at the right time and in the same condition I lent them to him. Just as neighbors borrow one another's bowls, cans, beds, and clothes, as well as money and money equivalents, I shall take nothing in return for this action.

5. We are not talking here about donating or gifting, or about buying or selling, or about *Zinskauf*.[2] But rather we speak of lending, with which usury nowadays does almost all its business—especially through lending money.

6. That is why this message should be diligently taught to the people. It requires no great smarts or high wisdom but is rather a very plain message and therefore very easy to comprehend. Namely, if someone lends something and takes in return something in excess of it or—which is the same thing—takes back something better, that constitutes usury. For lending means taking back no more than what was borrowed—just as the prophets and Christ himself teach us [Luke 6:34] and as worldly law codes also teach.

---

2 See the section on *Zinskauf,* p. 17.

DEALING WITH OBJECTIONS

First Objection

7. There are those nigglers pondering how it could potentially be acceptable—and more about this later—to take something more or better than one has lent. You pastors should listen to such people after your sermon or refer them to the lawyers. For lawyers are commanded to direct or instruct them because of their oath and office.

8. But your preaching should maintain that it is usury when anyone lends whatsoever and takes in return something more or better. Do not let this message abandon the pulpit or let yourself be forced to drop it because it is the right message—and also what all laws describe.

9. In cases requiring further explanation, individuals should seek advice from the pastor, privately and in confidence, or from the lawyers. For if you wanted to resolve from the pulpit everything on the topic of usury and its sophistries that was contrived and written earlier (and will continue to be conceived and written), the last days would likely arrive before we could ever begin preaching on usury.

Second Objection

10. Second, when someone shouts, "If this were so, usury would condemn almost the whole world, for such lending is now common in all estates," do not be fooled by such screaming, and do not even consider getting into an argument about our message. Instead, continue to preach it unperturbed, and send these shouters to me or my peers, or let them go to the appropriate lawyers to complain to them!

11. Tell them that it is your duty not to deviate from this message, and also tell them the pulpit is not the place to deal with everyone's objections. If they don't like to hear this, simply tell them that this message is not of your making and that therefore you are not obliged to interpret or bend it. Everyone is advised to consult their own conscience for advice or, as has already been said, go seek better explanations from the learned experts.

12. After all, attempts to testify together with the world against the law and the word of God are very lazy objections easily refuted by any village sexton. For what else is the world than wrongdoing, being stingy, and profiteering and indulging in all kinds of vices and malice?

So is it then not just platitude when one says that the world is evil and unfaithful, that it respects neither virtue nor honor and knows neither shame nor discipline? That is why you do not have to deflect this argument saying the whole world is like that. This does not require any learned doctor because any herding boy can tell you: the world does as it does, not as it should.

13. So spare us this excuse that the entire world is condemned. After all, it is neither new nor strange that the world is desperate, cursed, and condemned: it has always been like that and always will be. Following the world, you will follow it into the abyss of hell. That is why it is said, "Let justice be done though the world may perish."[3] One should precisely look at not what the horde or the world does but what is right to do and what they ought to do.

Third Objection

14. Third, someone might say, "If this were so, who would want to lend or help anyone else? Then I would rather, like others, keep my money, my grain, and my goods and not lend anything to anyone." To this I answer: of course, secular law does not compel you to lend, give, or sell to anyone. It does not punish you if you refrain. Unless, that is, in times of inflation or other hardship, when the authorities have to force farmers, citizens, and nobles to sell grain—if they have any—or forbid them to willfully inflict price hikes. Because the latter is exactly as if they were stealing and robbing in the market, stealing out of homes or out of wallets, for willfully inflicted price hikes turn plain selling into usurious action. (But that is too big a bite for right now.)

15. So first things first: let us first understand usury in the act of borrowing. Once we have mastered this—likely accomplished only after judgment day—then we shall want to teach another lesson exclusively on usury in commerce. There we will also explain what Christ correctly replied to this.

16. Meanwhile, do not let yourself be confused by such talk, but stay with this message and say that it is written: he who borrows and takes something in return for it—he is a usurer! Do not deviate from this message, even if a hundred thousand objections were raised! This objection, we should add, is just as lazy as the one first mentioned, and the same answer suffices here that we gave for the custom of the world.

---

3 Latin: *Fiat justitia et pereat mundus.*

17. Dear friend, what does it really mean when you say, "Who would possibly lend the way I demand it?" Is it not known that the world does nothing good? That God (as Ps 13 says), looking down from heaven at all children of men, cannot spot among them even one doing good? [Ps 14:2]? So what is new or strange when you say, "Who will want to lend to anyone for nothing?" After all, lending for nothing in return is a good work: that is why no one does it among the children of men. They do this instead: they lie, cheat, steal, seize, and rob. Where the sword cannot or does not defend it, children of men do as is their nature. The sword does not force them to do good: it only denies them, as much as it can manage, to do evil.

Fourth Objection

18. Fourth, Sir Usurer says, "Dear friend, given current times, I do a great service to my neighbor when I lend him at 5, 6, or 10 percent interest. He gratefully thanks me for such a loan as if it were a special treat; he even requests it from me. He himself volunteers to give me five, six, or ten gulden interest for every hundred gulden loaned. Should I not accept that with a clear conscience and without it being usury? Who would consider such a gift usury?"

To this I say: whosoever desires to boast, aggrandize, and whitewash, let them do it, but ignore them! Instead, you, preacher, stick to the message: with any loan, one should not demand more or better coin in return. Whosoever then takes more or better, this is usury and not "service." It harms his neighbor, just as robbing and stealing does.

19. Not all is a blessing and service to others that someone calls a service and a blessing. Even an adulteress and an adulterer do each other great service and pleasure. A horseman does great service to a murderer and arsonist when he helps him rob in the streets and attack land and people. Likewise, the papists do a great service to our folks if they do not drown, hang, burn, murder, or put to death in prison all Protestants but let at least some of them live to then "just" chase them away or "only" seize their possessions. Even the devil does his servants a great and immeasurable service, rendering much help and advice to them by making them into great and powerful lords.

20. In summary, every day the world is just filled with excellent services and benevolent deeds. Often even the pious must feel happy and consider it a blessing when they receive something from evil. The poets

report of a cyclops, Polyphemus, who—about to eat the entire group of adventurers traveling with Ulysses[4]—nonetheless wanted to show his kindness: he promised Ulysses he would express kindness by first eating all his journeymen and by choosing to eat him last. Yes, that too was a fine "service"—and so benevolent!

Nowadays, nobility and commoners, peasants and citizens also engage in similar "services" and "blessings": they buy up goods; withhold them from sale, thus causing price hikes; and increase the prices of grain, barley, and every basic need. Only then they act the innocent, saying, "Indeed, one must have what one must have; I commit my money to the people to serve them, although I could well and gladly keep it for myself."

21. God is deceived and declared a fool in this fine way, for how can that poor, merciful God observe here anything else but proud services, good works, and benevolence all around? He would bring himself not to let on about the foul stink surrounding them. For, before even he realized it, the children of men became so very holy. Somehow, the world suddenly ran out of usurers, stingy or evil people; rather, it is full of veritable saints, one serving the other and none ever doing damaging things to their neighbor.

22. Of this, preacher, you should speak and not keep silent. Explain to the people clearly and distinctly that nothing is called a "service" or "benevolent" that is done against the word of God and against the law. For it is said, "Thou shalt serve God alone!" [Matt 6:24 KJV—actually, "No man can serve two masters. . . . Ye cannot serve God and mammon."[5]]

Whatsoever does not serve his word or law may still be praised as a service and blessing, yet it serves and blesses a different god—namely, the devil. Again, therefore, he who lends and takes more or better in return is a usurer sinning against God. Should he indeed render a service, he does it to the dreaded devil. And that is despite many poor and needy men requiring such "service" and bringing themselves to accept as favor that they are not completely eaten alive.

---

4 The ancient Greek hero Ulysses (Odysseus) in Homer's *Odyssey*.
5 Contemporary translations often use the words *wealth* or *money* in place of *Mammon*. Luther uses *Mammon* throughout his text to indicate the idolatrous nature of an outright worship of money and wealth.

23. Likewise, a man must play along—most certainly with reluctance—when it is spun out to him as a "service" where great misery forced him to give 5 or more percent interest. But you who take this interest are neither safe nor excused. You are even worse if you regard such interest as your right and spin your taking as a "service" and "blessing." For you do not consider the interest payment a free gift, and you know that fact for sure. Even your conscience cannot deny this. You take his payment as the actual profit on lending your money.

24. After all, a gift is not actually a profit but a voluntary thing, freely given and received. But that does not happen in such a trade—and you know that. You may gloss it over; you may lie and call it a gift. But in truth, it is a profit and usury given to you by the needy one in his distress. And at times, he even has to put up with you misrepresenting your profit as a gift. He will put up with you as someone whom he otherwise considers a miser and nickel-nurser, not quite valuing you enough to afford you even a single casing of oat grain, let alone five or ten gulden on a loan of one hundred. Such a man would certainly not say that you did him a service. Instead, he does you—and is forced to do you—a service because he cannot get money in any other way.

* * *

REVIEW QUESTIONS

1. What is Luther's central message about usury?
2. Imagine that you ask to borrow your son's car for a trip to buy groceries. He lets you use it, and the gas tank is full when you take the car. Toward the end of your trip, you decide you need to refill what gas you consumed. Would you agree that this does not involve usury but is rather an example of true borrowing in Luther's sense? Why or why not?
3. Now imagine the following scenario: You want to borrow your son's car for a trip to buy groceries. The gas tank is near empty, and he is hesitant to give it to you. He then agrees to let you have it—if you completely fill up the gas tank. Is your son guilty of usury? Why or why not?
4. In your own words, summarize the four objections Luther addresses.

STUDY QUESTIONS

1. Luther distinguishes *lending* from *usury*. How would you apply this distinction in a world that has come to accept interest payments as a routine, legitimate part of doing business?

2. Luther's tone is often deliberately ironic (see, for example, paragraphs 20 and 21 above). Why do you think he used this technique? Would that work for contemporary pastors preaching on financial abuses? Why or why not?

3. In a 2009 interview, Lloyd Blankfein, then head of investment bank Goldman Sachs, described Goldman's banking business as "doing God's work."[6] Based on the four objections Luther raises, discuss what Luther might have replied to Blankfein.

* * *

---

6 Matt Phillips, "Goldman Sachs' Blankfein on Banking: 'Doing God's Work,'" MarketBeat, *Wall Street Journal*, November 9, 2009, https://www.wsj.com/articles/BL-MB-13358.

Part II

Make Use of the Lawyers

25. Now, it is not the world's way that she gives much, even if she is over-flowing. Nor is it her way to donate anything to friends who are poor or those in dire need. Ask yourself, then, How much less likely will someone give anything to you, of all people, when you are a rascal, a pariah, and—because of your greed and usury—commonly cursed, disreputable, and an insult?

26. But I am getting too far from the message: such arguments belong in private conversation. Still, you, preacher, confidently send this message from the pulpit: lending and taking more in return is usury. After that, answer them at your home if they want to insist on their opinions. Or refer them to the lawyers for them to reply with better explanations of the message.

27. In order that you yourself are not completely unprepared and people do not consider you an empty blister, you may, if you wish, con-sider my additional considerations of this trade.[1] However, it seems to me that, for the sake of your own peace and quiet, you better refer critics to the lawyers. Their office, as stated above, is to judge and teach in such worldly, passing, and miserable matters, especially for those who want to apply sophistry and nitpick against this message. For your part, you should absolutely insist on this message—namely, that lending and tak-ing more in return is usury!

28. All law and all lawyers will have to confirm this message not only according to the gospel (which does not concern the lawyers) but also according to their law books. That is why you cannot go wrong with

---

1 A reference to his earlier sermons on the topic. See footnotes 4, p. 2, and 15, p. 7.

this message. Let the legal explanation be as good or evil as it pleases, yet you have rightly preached against usury—namely, that lending does not mean taking back more in return or else it is usury, not lending.

A REAL-LIFE EXAMPLE

29. Here now is my additional instruction—in case you find it too difficult to endure peace and quiet, or if you also want to understand it better yourself.

30. And so it can happen and is frequently the case that I, Hans, lend to you, Baltzer,[2] a hundred gulden under the conditions that I get them back on Michaelis[3] to apply to my own obligations, or that I—should you become a defaulter—suffer damage. Michaelis now comes, and you do not return my hundred gulden. Then the judge will grab me by the collar, throw me in the tower or prison, or some similar calamity or another besets me until I pay my own debts. I am stuck, unable to make a living or change my lot. I suffer this great disadvantage because you were delinquent and rewarded me badly for my good deed.

THE CASE FOR *SCHADEWACHT*

31. Now, what should I do here? My damage grows while you remain delinquent and asleep. And every day, new costs and damage come to me as long as you continue sleeping on while in default. Who should bear the damage here, who should pay for it? Because *Mr. Schadewacht*[4]—that is, my damage, increasing day and night—will remain present as an intolerable guest in my house until I am utterly ruined.

32. Let's first talk worldly and judicially about the matter; we'll save theology for later! In this case, you, Baltzer, are liable to give me all the additional money that *Mr. Schadewacht* costs me on top of the principal of the original loan. After all, it is your fault that you left me like this; it is just as if you deliberately had taken that money from me. That is why it is just and matches reason as well as natural law that you give everything back to me—both the principal and the damage. After all, I lent

---

2 Baltzer: a reduced form of "Balthazar," a first name.

3 *Michaelis*: colloquial name for the holiday to honor Saint Michael, observed on September 29. Also *Michaelmas*.

4 For an explanation of the concept, see p. 18.

you the hundred gulden not to ruin myself or allow you to ruin me but rather to help you without myself being harmed. All this is so clear and evident that even if all the law and lawyers' books should go missing, reason would still have to recognize it—as weak as that reason may ever turn out to be.

33. In Latin language, law books call such *Schadewacht* "compensation."[5] And such a loan is obviously not usury but a straight, laudable, and honest service, a good work to the neighbor. Moreover, if the person is a Christian, it is also a Christian work that God will reward not only here on earth, as God does toward worldly good works, but also in that other world. Thus, David says in Psalms, "They will be remembered forever"[6] [Ps 112:6]. God will never forget a Christian's good work. He pays the worldly good works here on earth, and after that, they are forgotten. Therefore, jurisprudence and secular rule can do no more than teach and support such worldly and transitory good works.

DAMAGE THROUGH MISSED BUSINESS OPPORTUNITIES

34. To this *Schadewacht* we can add another variant. Imagine that you, Baltzer, do not give me my hundred gulden on Michaelis. Imagine further that a purchasing opportunity presents itself to me at the same time—such as buying a garden or field, a house, or something else at a bargain price. Such an opportunity would provide great benefits and livelihood for me and my children. But now I have to forego this opportunity. Your delinquency and indifference damage me in that they prevent me from taking advantage of such a bargain purchase. If I had not lent you my one hundred gulden but kept them at home, then I could now pay half of it to cover the legal cost and buy the garden with the other half. But since I lent it to you, you are doubling my damage: I can neither pay here nor buy there and thus suffer damage on both sides. This is called "double damage: a real loss and a missed gain."[7]

35. One must then let the lawyers argue over whether the same hundred gulden have caused damage only once or indeed twice through a lost

---

5 Luther uses the Latin *interesse*. It is related in meaning but different from the English word *interest*. He uses Latin here to communicate the concept of indemnity, compensation, or reparation at the core of *Schadewacht*.

6 Latin: *in memoria aeterna erit iustus*.

7 Latin: *duplex interest, damni emergentis et lucri cessantis*.

business opportunity. For if Hans himself, at the time of the potential damage, owes a hundred gulden, then there is only one type of loss, for no one can, at the same time, pay his own debt with one hundred gulden and, on the other hand, buy the garden with those same one hundred gulden. However, if Hans himself owes only fifty gulden, then double damage may occur. It should also be noted whether the garden was, in fact, already on sale at the time Hans loaned out his hundred gulden because what is not for sale nobody can buy, not even with cash on hand. Also, one must see that Hans could well have lost the hundred gulden through theft, robbers, fire, and the like so that, for such reason, he would not have been able to pay or buy.

36. Money is just an uncertain and fickle thing on which one cannot reliably build transactions! Countless similar circumstances or coincidences must therefore be considered by the lawyers, lest the *Schadewacht* in the end turn rogue or into usury. Even wise people may be mistaken in this because, after all, how can one make everything so pure with that impure law the world requires in this miserable life? Having a coarse, bad, and simplistic law will suffice. For it cannot be subtle and sharp, or it gets such nicks that it cannot even cut butter anymore, even though it should split chunks into logs. Compared to this, Christ and his gospel remain a different thing altogether.

37. But you, preacher, have heard enough of this to know what usury is. Namely, if Baltzer did not return the hundred gulden on Michaelis and Hans himself owed in the meantime—that is, suffered damage—then Baltzer should refund him the monetary damage incurred through payment delay, as legislated under secular law. If he also prevented Hans from buying the garden, then Baltzer—if Hans wants to be tough with him—has to add something more. But it is best if they both negotiate and settle it like good friends because it is difficult and dangerous to estimate the monetary damage accurately and correctly. This is especially so, since the purchase was not actually made, and it was not even decided how expensive the garden would have been if bought and if not maybe another garden just as good might be found. On the other hand, in the case of the secondary damage incurred by Hans due to his own late payment, the expenses can easily be calculated. By contrast, the gospel, as we will see, would have addressed this in a much simpler way.

Payments for Hypothetical Damage

38. But look and well take notice, my dear pastor, that such a loan that causes a real loss does not occur in contemporary dealings. Mostly, these loans are just veritable usury: after usurious lenders heard that Hans has suffered damage with his lending of a hundred gulden and now reasonably demands the reimbursement of his damage, they brazenly and indiscriminately added two gulden *Schadewacht* payment to every one hundred gulden they loaned—one for paying the expenses incurred and another for the missed garden purchase.

39. They just act as if one hundred gulden had naturally grown an attachment of such two gulden *Schadewacht*. So to any one hundred gulden they lend out, they automatically add a charge of two gulden for the damage. In effect, they claim reimbursement for damage they have never suffered at all. For just because you, lender, own one hundred gulden, it does not follow that you actually have to repay any debt on Michaelis. And it also does not follow that there is any garden on offer that you could buy on Michaelis. But you just add these two fake damages to your safe and secure one hundred gulden. Every year anew, you take five, six, ten gulden just as if you were such a Hans, who would have been brought into default and constraints by his Baltzer.

40. No, do you hear, you are not the same Hans because there is no Baltzer here who makes you such a Hans! You make up and pretend that you would be such a Hans—without any Baltzer whatsoever. That is why you are a usurer! You even make your neighbor's money replace your fictitious damage, even though no one has actually done damage to you and even though you can neither prove nor quantify it. The lawyers call such damage "an untrue damage that one dreams up by oneself."[8]

41. "Yes," you say, "but it is possible and could well happen that my hundred gulden will eventually suffer such a double damage." And you are right. Therefore, let us negotiate on this very basis. At some point, I could have to give you the five or six gulden as compensation for actual damage. Until then, though, let me hold on to these guldens for the time being. That is, as long as your hundred gulden do not suffer such double damage, I will not give you anything. On that basis, we agree on the matter, and this is a just loan. It is wrong to say that there could be potential damage and that, therefore, I might perhaps be able to neither

---

8 Latin: *non verum, sed fantasticum interesse.*

pay nor buy. Instead, it must mean that damage was indeed done, and as a consequence, I could not actually pay or buy.

42. Otherwise it would mean "Creating from something that is not something that must be"[9]—that is, creating from what is uncertain a veritable and certain thing. Would not such usury devour the world in just a few years?

SUMMARY

43. In summary, it is now sufficiently explained that lending means to take in return nothing in excess of what was loaned and that it shall occur for the service or benefit of the needy. Stick to this message!

44. It is also easy to comprehend that compensating damages must not exceed the borrowed sum. It means neither giving nor taking in excess of the actual damage because the misfortune from which he has to recover strikes the lender at random and outside his control. But in the actual dealings, it is often the exact opposite. Here, one party pursues and invents damage at the expense of his needy neighbor, wants to fatten himself with it and become rich, lazy, and squander idly, thus boasting through other people's labor, worry, peril, and damage. And so as lender, I sit behind my stove and let my hundred gulden work for me out in the lands. And yet I keep them because it is money lent and therefore safe for me without any worry of peril. Dear friend, who would not want to enjoy that?

45. What has been said here of borrowed money shall also apply to borrowed grain, wine, and like goods, since they may likewise experience such double damage. But such damages should not be considered as naturally attached to these goods but likewise may happen accidentally. Therefore, they cannot be counted as damage until there is proof that the damage actually happened. Where damage is claimed and compensation taken without such proof, one should know that this is usury and injustice. Establishing when and where such damage occurs is best done according to guidance from lawyers because pondering the countless circumstances is a vast and never-ending story. It would indeed be best to negotiate and settle the matter through referees or good friends.

---

9 Latin: *ex contingente necessarium.*

46. That is how to do this justly and peacefully. Because, as Aristotle teaches,[10] no law can be so sophisticated as to cover all possible coincidences or circumstances. But were such a law ever invented, according to the words of the smartest of Romans, Scipio, it is sure to also be the greatest injustice: "The tighter the law, the vaster the injustice!"[11] Or too sharp gets blunted! That is why you have to give in on both sides, and let equity be the master of all justice.

* * *

REVIEW QUESTIONS

1. Luther suggests that pastors refer the critics of his message to jurists (the "lawyers"). Why does he suggest that?
2. Describe the concept of *Schadewacht* in your own words. Where have you seen the concept of indemnity applied in today's economy?
3. Review the idea of "double damage" caused by delinquency. What contemporary examples could you imagine or did you encounter?

STUDY QUESTIONS

1. In explaining the real-life example, Luther proves that he understands quite well how the perspective of the gospel collides with worldly law. Did you expect such insight in a "religious" tract? Why or why not? Would you expect your pastor to be able to preach in such a way? Why or why not?
2. For their consumer credits, many credit card companies charge interests that are routinely some 15 to 25 percent above the going rate set by the Federal Reserve. Some argue that the rate has to be high because they serve "high-risk" borrowers, and their loans are constantly at risk of default. However, many of their clients never default yet have to pay the elevated rate.

---

10 Aristotle, *Nicomachean Ethics*, trans. W. D. Ross, book 5, Internet Classics Archive, http://classics.mit.edu/Aristotle/nicomachaen.5.v.html.
11 Latin: *summum ius, summa iniura.*

Compare this situation to the idea of "hypothetical damage" Luther discusses beginning in paragraph 38.

3. Reconsider the previous question. Since the financial crisis in 2008/2009 and at least until 2021, the federal rate was close enough to zero to make interest of little consequence. Inflation, until recently, was also not high enough to matter much. This means that borrowers from the Federal Reserve—like banks—could borrow money practically for free. Yet the interest rates of many credit card companies never reflected this. Would this change the case Luther makes that "he who lends and takes more or better in return is a usurer"? Why or why not?

* * *

Part III

Laws Alone Are Insufficient: They Must Be Taught

47. All this is legal, and the lawyers should teach it! But since they are not preachers, it remains hidden and buried in their books and does not get out to the people. Therefore, we preachers have to talk about it and warn, unless we want to be Antinomians[1] and, through someone else's sin, join the world going to hell. This does not mean the lawyers are excused from doing their part. Lawyers reading in schools should diligently teach that to the youth! And those working in the courts should inform the parties in earnest! Then surely a little more of it would circulate among the people.

48. But even more should lawyers teach who serve as chancellors and councilors at court because then this insight could and should descend from the top down to the very lowest level. But if those lawyers up there are silent or holding back, then our shouting as poor little preachers down here will accomplish little. For where we convert one person, they spoil many thousands.

49. After our preaching, therefore, the fight against usury, with all its sins, remains the fight of the jurists. Because our fence will not stop the flood if those tasked to guard the dam do not help our effort. Anyone should consider how to protect their conscience in his walk of life![2] We preachers can advise instantly and easily because none or only a few will follow us.

---

1 Hotspurs against the (any) law.
2 "His walk of life" could also be translated more literally as "his status and office."

THE WORLD CANNOT BE WITHOUT USURY

50. They say the world cannot be without usury. That is certainly true, for no regimen in the world is or was so tough and strict that it could fend off all sin. Even if any regimen could contain all sin, original sin remains—the source of all sins and including the devil (of which lawyers are not expected to know anything)—and it must be fought anew daily and with utmost vigor.

51. Therefore, the world cannot be without usury, without avarice, without pride, without fornication, without adultery, without murder, without stealing, without blasphemy, and without all kinds of sin. Otherwise, it would not be the world or would be a world without the world, a devil without the devil.

Whether this excuses them they will learn right here. The Lord says, "Occasions for stumbling are bound to come, but woe to the one by whom the stumbling block comes!" [Matt 18:7]. Usury, then, must exist—but woe to the usurers!

WE MUST ACTIVELY FIGHT USURY

52. Secular law is a feeble, second-rate, and unclean law, which preserves the temporal peace and the belly's life only in wimpy fashion; only for the sake of the saints it multiplies and nourishes humanity toward eternal life. Therefore, secular law cannot fend off all and every sin beyond what is actually possible. Even a shepherd cannot keep all sheep from the wolf, from plague and other diseases. Nevertheless, he should fight back where he can and allow neither wolf nor disease to reign freely. In the same way, secular government should not allow any room for sin but fight it most rigorously. Enough sin will remain despite the government's will.

53. What was said above remains true: the world cannot be without usury, not without murder or adultery. This just cannot be prevented, and before you know it, it has already happened. Incidentally, if one were able to prevent it from the outset, one would need no law, nor the lawyers or princes. But since one cannot prevent it, one should at least manage it: past evil should be punished, and future evil—as far as possible—should be deterred.

54. It is the same with usury: one cannot fully stop usury. But if it occurs or grows so fast that it gets the upper hand, finally turning

shameless and wanting to be counted as a virtue, then it can and must be curbed and controlled. Murder and adultery also happen; forbid them all you want. But if they want to happen and powerfully rip into society, such calamity forces us to control and fight them vigorously. The same must happen to all other vices: if they tear into society despite all prohibition, they must be confronted with force.

USURY IS NOT A NEW PROBLEM

55. When, at the time of Duke William,[3] the noblemen had become so proud that they defied their local prince and withheld land and chateaus from him, he had to force them out, storm their castles, and tear them down. This is what historians and lawyers already know: "From good manners arises good law, but good laws give rise to bad manners because law is the measure of what is forgiven. Inventing law also coinvented the fraud of that law."[4]

56. Malice forces us to intervene by applying good law, yet all malice happens despite good law. The world cannot be any different—and does not want to be—because external order, without the Holy Spirit and mercy, can only be upheld through law and coercion.

57. Therefore, it is necessary that God governs, especially where secular government cannot help or is itself evil—that is, it does not want to help (like, unfortunately, is now mostly the case in German lands). Or where government even conducts itself so that people say neither honor nor virtue remains in many princely states but especially among cardinals and bishops. There, God must govern just as he did with Sodom, with the flood, with Babylon, with Rome, and with other cities where he raged to destroy them. We Germans want it done likewise: we do not stop raving until one can say Germany is gone like Rome and Babylon.

---

3 Duke Wilhelm III of Saxony, "The Brave," born April 30, 1425, in Meißen and died September 17, 1482, in Weimar.

4 Latin: *ex malis moribus bonae leges funt, econtra, ex honis legibus mali mores funt, quia lex est virtus peccati, inventa lege inventa est fraus legis*—"*lex est virtus peccati*"; literally, "law is the virtue of sin."

Usury in Ancient Greece

58. Thus, we read of usury that in the time of Solon,[5] the city of Athens was so corrupt that not only was land overloaded with interest, but the citizens themselves had to sell their bodies into bondage to the usurers. As a result, Solon issued a law forbidding people to make new slaves and to take any usurious interest on real estate. Moreover, he limited usury so that one could not give more than the Centesima[6]—that is, one one-hundredth, or 1 percent. Paying at that rate, in a hundred months, enough interest was paid to equal the principal sum.

59. According to our calculations, this means an interest payment of twelve gulden per year on a loan of a hundred gulden—one gulden each month since they took interest on a monthly basis. Through this law, Solon liberated many citizens, and many properties became debt-free again. Aristotle also writes[7] that a pious man called Oxylus had determined that no usurious interest should be paid from the underlying land. It is also said of the great Alexander[8] that he paid usury interest of over fifty-nine tons of gold in order to ransom some of his warriors. In the end, he too had to tame usury.

60. This is what usury does when the princes and lords are not on their guard. In a short time, before you know it, usury grows and rises so much that it soon eats and devours the whole land and all the goods, so that in the end, you have no choice but to intervene and fight it by force.

---

5 Solon was a statesman, lawmaker, and poet living circa 630–560 BCE in ancient Greece, in the city-state of Athens. Luther refers here to Solon's efforts to legislate against political and economic, as well as moral, decline.

6 A term from Roman law: literally, "the hundredth part." The Romans, however, calculated interest rates *per month* (!). By contrast, we use the calendar year, as, for example, in the annual percentage rate (APR). Centesima thus means 1 percent of the principal was due each month (!). This translates to simple annual interest rate of 12 percent and an APR of 12.68 percent—including compound interest. See paragraph 89.

7 Aristotle, *Politics*, trans. Benjamin Jowett, book 6, Internet Classics Archive, http://classics.mit.edu/Aristotle/politics.html.

8 A reference to Alexander the Great. Alexander III of Macedon was born July 20 or 21, 356 BCE, and died June 10 or 11, 323 BCE. His war campaigns led him from Greece to as far as present-day Pakistan.

This has happened in our time, and it still happens through the traders and their cartels,[9] which just about devoured all of Germany. Oh, if only God would give us a Solon or an Alexander who would control and resist usury! Amen.

* * *

REVIEW QUESTIONS

1. Why is it important that lawyers, especially those working in government, educate and teach about the law on usury?
2. What would remain even if the government could make laws controlling all sinful behavior?

STUDY QUESTIONS

1. Luther uses a Latin quote to describe an unusual effect of existing law: "From good manners arises good law, but good laws give rise to bad manners because law is the measure of what is forgiven. Inventing law also coinvented the fraud of that law." Discuss contemporary examples of this.
2. Luther blames the situation in his time on "traders and their cartels." The Fuggers, for example, made their fortune as personal bankers and financiers of dukes, princes, kings, emperors, and popes. During the sixteenth century, the Fugger family was allowed a near total monopoly on the European copper trade. Today, where have you noticed examples of cartels, monopolies, or, more generally, collusion among businesses to the disadvantage of consumers?
3. A recent study in the United Kingdom found that out of a population of sixty-seven million, over one million people are in debt to illegal and unregulated money lenders.[10] Amid the economic fallout of austerity and the pandemic, false "friends" turn acquaintances into revenue streams—and thus become "loan

---

9 For more context on *cartels* (*Gesellschaften*), see p. 1.
10 The study mentioned is aptly titled "Swimming with Sharks: Tackling Illegal Money Lending in England," Centre for Social Justice, March 2022, https://www.centreforsocialjustice.org.uk/library/swimming-with-sharks.

sharks." The vast majority of their victims already owe money to legal creditors and are on benefits or use food banks. Almost half told interviewers that the everyday cost of living—not surprise bills—drove them to accept crippling terms that would trap them into never-ending debt. Discuss the role of "shadow lenders" in the context of usury. Have you seen this happen in your circle of friends and acquaintances? What do payday lenders and check-cashing outfits do, and how do they make their money?

* * *

Part IV

Usury in Ancient Rome

61. Likewise, in the history of the Romans, we read that when usury took over at Rome, two men—Valerius Publicola[1] and M. Rutilius—were commissioned to tame it. They paid the interest partly from public funds and partly—perhaps to avoid turmoil and other inconveniences—at the expense of the debtors. After that, they soon appointed a taskmaster called Genutius to enforce that henceforth, usury was disallowed.

Once, a rich fellow named Papyrius wanted to shamefully disgrace a lad after he became a slave to him as a result of usury. A law was then passed that forbade the enslavement of anyone, so that no one may become a serf through usury.

62. But when usury became so bad that a rebellion arose, and the people demonstrated in the city, chief Roman tax lawyer, Hortensius, had to confront usury. This can be found in Titus Livius.[2] When the first Emperor Julius found out that usury had gone too high, he decreed that lenders had to apply all previously received usury against paying down the principal.

Shortly before him, Cicero, when he was governor in Asia, defeated usury by declaring that one should give only one Centesima a month, or 12 percent annually. Previously, one had to give four Centesimae—that is,

---

1 Publius Valerius Publicola (or Poplicola) was a Roman aristocrat who died 503 BCE. In *The Federalist Papers*, authors Alexander Hamilton, James Madison, and John Jay used "Publius" as their pseudonym in honor of Publicola's role in establishing the Roman Republic.

2 Titus Livius (59 BCE–CE 17). An example of a contemporary edition of his writings is Titus Livius, *The History of Rome* (London: Forgotten Books, 2018). A digital and searchable edition of 1857 is available online at the Perseus Digital Library at Tufts University, http://www.perseus.tufts.edu/hopper/.

four gulden each month, or 48 percent annually, for a loan of one hundred gulden. For the same reason, Brutus's steward also locked up Salamin's council members inside city hall, starving several of them to death.

63. The law books also show how often it has been forbidden to take what is now called compound interest.[3] In situations where usurious interest exceeds double the principal, one should not take anything more.

64. It turns out, then, that usury at all times caused much heartache and that all the pious, praiseworthy princes and lords have dealt with it. Likewise, all wise and reasonable heathen branded usury as extremely bad. Thus, for example, Aristotle[4] states that usury is against nature because it always takes more than it gives and because it invalidates the rational standard of all virtue, which is called "equal for equal."[5]

65. He continues, saying money is, by nature, unfruitful and does not multiply by itself. Wherever it seemingly multiplies on its own, as it does in usury, this is against the nature of money, for money is not alive. Nor does money bear like a tree or a field—both of which each year provide in excess of what they are because they do not lie idle and without fruit, as the gulden by its very nature does. Also, in *Ethics* 4,[6] he writes that usurers are shameful tinkerers,[7] a role Saint Paul sharply forbade for bishops [1 Tim 3:2–3; Titus 1:7].

66. Saint Paul says the usurer takes where he is not supposed to and takes more than he should. But that means robbing and fattening himself in a shameful way. Those taking from other people, who steal or rob, we call them thieves and robbers, and we usually hang them from the

---

3 That is, interest on interest. Latin: *usuras usurarum*.

4 Aristotle, *Politics*, trans. Benjamin Jowett, book 1, Internet Classics Archive, http://classics.mit.edu/Aristotle/politics.html.

5 Luther is quoting a common saying, which WA states as unconfirmed: *aequalitas arithmetica* (arithmetic equality). The meaning of it would be to ensure that a benefit and the compensation for it ought to be kept in a fair balance, often expressed arithmetically.

6 Aristotle, *Nicomachean Ethics*, trans. W. D. Ross, book 5, Internet Classics Archive, http://classics.mit.edu/Aristotle/nicomachaen.5.v.html.

7 "Tinkerer," for the German *Hantierer*, means someone who handles something, but the dominant connotation is that they manipulate it while doing so. In Luther's Bible translation of 1524, for example, Titus 1:7 then translates as "Not a dishonest tinkerer." Many English translations likewise require a bishop to be "not eager for dishonest gain." Thus, 1 Tim 3:2–3 seems to be translated as "Not a lover of money"—a different connotation than "dishonest tinkerer" suggests.

gallows. But although the usurer is just such a thief and robber, he sits securely in his chair, which is why he is also called a swivel-chair bandit.[8]

67. Roman senator Cato, that great and serious enemy of all vices, writes at the beginning of his book praising agriculture, "Our ancestors held this view and embodied it in their laws, that the thief be punished double and the usurer fourfold."[9] That is why one can guess, he says, how much more they despise usurers over thieves. The same Cato also wrote, "Dear friend, what is usury other than murder?" So that is what the heathen said and did!

USURY IN THE BIBLICAL ACCOUNT

68. What, then, are we Christians supposed to do? Just applying reason, the heathen have been able to gauge that a usurer is a fourfold thief and murderer. But we Christians honor them so much that we worship them for their money's sake. We pay no attention to the mockery and great harm that does to the name of Christianity and Christ himself.

69. Even if we were not Christians, reason should tell us—like it did tell the heathen—that a usurer is a murderer. Because, after all, whosoever takes away someone's livelihood, who robs and steals, commits as great a murder as he who kills by starving someone to death.

70. For that is what a usurer does—and all the while, he sits securely in his chair, where by all means he should hang on the gallows. He should be eaten by as many ravens as he has stolen gulden—provided there is ever enough flesh on him that matching numbers of ravens could participate. Meanwhile, one hangs the little thieves who have only stolen the fewest of gulden. Even Cato, the enemy of usurers, says, "Little thieves lay trapped in stocks, while the great thieves walk in gold and silken splendor." Therefore, it will undoubtedly happen that in the end, we will suffer and atone alongside the usurers because we neither punish nor thwart them.

71. But enough of talking about the heathen! Let us read from Nehemiah [5:11]! There we read how the Jews, upon returning from Babylon, in their need had to give their brothers the Centesima[10] as monthly

8 German: *Stuhlräuber*. See our explanation of derogatory terms, p. 16.
9 Cato the Elder, *On Agriculture*, trans. W. D. Hooper and Harrison Boyd Ash, Loeb Classical Library, vol. 283 (Cambridge, MA: Harvard University Press, 1934), 2–3, https://www.loebclassics.com/view/cato-agriculture/1934/pb_LCL283.3.xml.
10 For Centesima, see footnote 6, p. 42.

interest. Such an old thing and such a misery is this concept of monthly interest, called Centesima, that it seems the heathen later took this concept from the Jews because the Jews count all their feasts, timed deals, and other affairs in units of months.

72. But it may also be that the Jews learned it from the heathen at the time of Nehemiah, for Nehemiah lived long before the Romans and Alexander reigned—over three hundred years before Christ's birth. If one were to doubt the existence of Centesimae among the Jews, there is a convincing interpretation in that text. Nehemiah says there, "The former governors who were before me laid heavy burdens on the people, and took food and wine from them, besides forty shekels[11] of silver" [Neh 5:15].

73. Now, forty shekels make exactly ten gulden, for each shekel is a quarter gulden. Let us imagine that grain, oil, and wine have accounted for about two or more gulden, for a total of ten plus two equals twelve gulden a year, or one gulden every month—that is exactly Centesima, or 1 percent of interest per month.

74. And when the people mourned and cried miserably, that pious prince, Nehemiah, intervened anew. He berated the usurers and ordered them to desist from taking 1 percent monthly usury and to return all fields, houses, vineyards, and everything they had acquired through their usury. Since the prince was in the grace of God, the people obeyed and followed him, and the calamity of usury stopped as was urgently needed.

75. He controlled usury, forced into action by the people's misery. The people were already sucked so dry that they could not help it anymore: although they had only just and with great difficulty been released from debt slavery, they sold themselves and their daughters and sons right back to the heathen.

* * *

---

11 The shekel mentioned here is a biblical unit of weight, not the Israeli currency. For an in-depth discussion of use and actual weight, see Nicola Ialongo and Giancarlo Lago, "A Small Change Revolution: Weight Systems and the Emergence of the First Pan-European Money," *Journal of Archaeological Science* 129 (May 1, 2021): 105379, https://doi.org/10.1016/j.jas.2021.105379.

REVIEW QUESTIONS

1. In paragraph 66, Luther calls usurers "swivel-chair bandits." What does this term imply?
2. Why are usurers considered murderers?

STUDY QUESTIONS

1. Beginning with paragraph 55, Luther teaches us about the history of usury. A common measure Luther advocates in his writings is legislation capping maximum interest rates that can be charged on a line of credit or loan. Some German towns implemented such usury laws in Luther's time. Today, more than half of all US states have usury laws in place, each dictating its own maximum legal limit. Research this topic and discuss the pros and cons of usury laws.
2. In paragraph 63, Luther quotes a law stating that debtors who had paid twice the principal amount in interest should owe no more payments. Take, for example, a credit card company today that made a loan at 18 percent interest. At that rate, interest payments accumulate to the amount of the principal after just four years. Provided that the debtor paid interest faithfully and never repaid any of the principal, that company should close the loan after eight years of payments. For by Luther's logic, they already received back their principal plus 100 percent interest through the debtor's interest payments alone and should not insist on getting more. What do you think would be the consequences if such practice became law in your jurisdiction?
3. Luther quotes Aristotle's old concept of the "infertility of money": money, on its own, is a dead object that cannot procreate any more than a rock will. Instead, it is the fruits of nature or the fruits of human labor, bought with money, that grow it. Only then does money grow, indirectly, by first producing new goods or growing fruit or grain and then selling them for more money than was initially paid to start the process. Discuss the merit of this idea. Does this make sense to you? Why or why not?
4. In paragraph 67, Luther quotes law, even before Roman times, as decreeing that thieves should be punished double but usurers quadruple. Why do you think such laws were made even in

antiquity? Why would usurers' crimes be punished more severely than thieves'?

5. In paragraph 75, Luther reports that people desperate for money had to sell themselves, their sons, or their daughters. Do you think this would be possible today? Why or why not?

* * *

Part V

Usury in Germany

76. We Germans could use such a Nehemiah right now! And if things do not change, then a Nehemiah must come—or Germany, with all its princes and lords, its lands and peoples, will become slaves to the usurers! After all, usury, over the past twenty or even ten years, has spread so much that any closer inspection makes you want for your heart to stop. And still usury increases, devours and swallows up incessantly; the longer, the more gruesome.

77. I learned that now on every Leipzig market, they take ten gulden, which is 30 percent per annum! Many add that people now even take 40 percent on the Naumburg markets. Maybe it is even more, I do not know. Shame on you! Where the devil does this lead in the end? These are not just monthly interest or Centesimae, also 12 percent a year; they are Trecentesime[1] and more, so three gulden and seven groschen[2] in a month. This is not annual interest, and neither is it monthly interest. This is weekly interest—genuine daily Jewish usury.[3]

---

1 Three times a Centesimus.

2 Usually 20 groschen per gulden, although amounts varied by jurisdiction and over time. Taking interest of 3 gulden, 7 groschen therefore makes 3.35 gulden—thus Luther states, "Trecentesime and more."

3 One of Luther's condemnable attacks on "the Jews." He refers here to a common occupation among medieval Jewry as professional money lenders—allegedly always at cutthroat rates. Money lending was, however, one of the few professions not forbidden for Jews by ubiquitous common legislation at the time and, unsurprisingly, became a common occupation. Furthermore, since canon law forbade Christians from usury, Jews in the Middle Ages were often put (or forced) into positions of middlemen acting as usurers to facilitate profit-making by Christian bankers, businessmen, kings, and so on. This, of course, only further increased Christian resentments against the Jews.

78. Therefore, whoever lends out one hundred gulden at Leipzig now takes 40 percent annual interest—that is, he devours a peasant or citizen in one year. If he lends out a thousand gulden, he takes four hundred gulden each year in interest—that is, he devours a knight or rich nobleman in one year. If he lends out ten thousand, he takes four thousand gulden a year in interest—that is, he eats a rich squire in a year. If he has a hundred thousand, as must be the case with the great trading houses, he takes forty thousand of annual interest—that is, he devours a great, rich prince in one year. If he has ten times a hundred thousand, he takes four hundred thousand a year—that is, a large king eaten in a year.

79. All the while, he suffers no danger, neither in body nor in goods; he does not work but sits behind the stove and roasts apples. Overall, such swivel-chair robbers can sit comfortably at home and devour the entire world in ten years. Now, there should be a Nehemiah here, a Solon, or an Alexander who would need to accomplish truly princely tasks!

80. But you clergymen and preachers, too, should think in this way and preach this to your princes and lords! Stimulate and urge them to control such devils and save the poor! Tell the lawyers to do likewise! For I write this to you pastors, above all else, to remind you of your office, because otherwise, I am almost ready to despair on this matter. Let us save our own conscience! As stated above, let us not condemn ourselves to hell through the sins of others! Also, the usurers need to know so at least some of them feel a guilty conscience and come to recognize their damned condition that rages against God, law, reason, and nature.

HELP FROM AUTHORITIES

81. Whether the princes can help here, I do not know. Usury is already too high and too deep, too far and too wide and, in any case, widely used and is by now perhaps simply accepted from continuing too long. Petty usurers as well as those charging compound interest can be expected to shout that everyone still has to fulfil their contracts.[4] Lawyers, however, have long since responded to this in detail: "In case of bad promises . . ."[5] Theologians concur. Even if they were written in blood, many such

---

4 Literally, "keep everything under hand and seal."
5 Latin: *in malis promissis recinde fidem*; "in case of bad promises, annul the promise."

contracts were given to the devil anyway: because what is against God, law, and nature, that is null and void!

82. Therefore, any prince who is able to should proceed with zeal, since he has license to annul contracts! He should tear them up and he should not care if his honor or belief is contested for it! Because upholding honor and advancing good faith is to obey God and keep one's faith and vows to him. Conversely, it means acting against honor and not acting in good faith if he does not tear up such letters and seals although he is permitted to do so.

83. Nehemiah provides a beautiful and convincing example of this. Beyond tearing up the contracts, he also takes away from the usurers all the grifted[6] fields, vineyards, olive groves, houses, and the Centesimae. In doing so, he probably does too little inasmuch as he does not force the usurers to return or refund all the property they stole and robbed by their usury in excess of what is considered customary. God also requires the usurers to return these goods, or at least, they are obliged to return them for God's sake. Because God is not satisfied with just letting go of usury; he also wants former usurers to reconcile with their neighbors and to see them mutually forgive one another's sins.

What We Clergymen Need to Do

84. Because this is what God wants, we let the princes do here what they can or are ready to do. Yet it is improper for us preachers to celebrate this. Let us be bishops in this regard; that is, keenly watch out and over this because our own salvation is on the line [Acts 20:28–31].

85. First, we should scold and condemn usury in the pulpit and repeat this message diligently and frankly, as we said above—namely, who lends something and takes more or better in return, he is a usurer and damned like a thief, robber, and murderer.

86. Second, if you know for sure about someone being a usurer, you should neither give him the sacrament nor grant him absolution until he repents! Otherwise, you will share in his usury and his sins, and you, too, will go to hell with him for the sake of his sins—even if, on account of your own sins, you should be as pure and holy as Saint John the

---

6 For German *erwucherten*, "obtained by means of usury."

Baptist. For as we know, Saint Paul says to Timothy, "Do not lay hands on[7] anyone hastily, and do not participate in the sins of others" [1 Tim 5:22]. Likewise, Romans says, "They know God's decree, that those who practice such things deserve to die—yet they not only do them but even applaud others who practice them" [Rom 1:32].

87. Third, ensure you are leaving the usurer to die like a heathen, and do not bury him among other Christians! Also, do not accompany him to the gravesite unless he has repented before he died! For if you do this, nevertheless, you make yourself partake of his sins as has been said above. This is because he is a usurer and thus an idol worshipper who is unbelieving because he serves Mammon. He therefore cannot have or receive forgiveness of sins, and he can have or receive neither the grace of Christ nor the communion of saints. He has condemned, isolated, and excommunicated himself as long as he does not plead guilty and repent.

88. Such words may be harsh to some. Maybe they will scare others too. Above all, they will sound terrifying to all those petty usurers who take only 5 or 6 percent. But you cannot make it tough enough for those big devourers of the world who can never get a percentage high enough because their loyalty is to Mammon and the devil. They make us scream and do not even care. About these, in particular, I have therefore said that in life and in death they should be left to the devil and not share in any Christian fellowship—which obviously seems to be how they themselves want to have it.

89. Then they claim we priests ourselves just want to be masters and thus move against them violently. For this is what now some noble clod-hoppers[8] and probably also some arrogant citizens and wealthy village boors yell about. Whenever we preachers do not preach what they want to hear, they are quick to say that we ourselves want to be their masters. These rude and nonnoble noblemen, these city rascals and rude village dupes have not even learned so much that they can tell the difference between the word of God being preached and the person of the preacher who preaches it.

90. Whenever the Word rebukes them, it must have been the teacher's own doing, they claim. Just as they desire to prevent the preaching of

---

7 Luther quotes from the Greek here; some contemporary translations, including the New Revised Standard Version (NRSV), interpret this to mean "Do not ordain . . ."

8 See explanation of Luther's derogatory terms, p. 16.

God's word in this way, they themselves believe they completely gobbled up that gospel already. Why are you fools angry with the pastor? Rather, be angry with your own wickedness, or be angry with God, whose Word scolds your evildoing! He will surely drive out your anger!

91. Therefore, if such usurers want to be angry with you when you withhold their absolution, reject giving them the sacrament, and refuse to bury them as Christians—just send them to the lawyers, and obtain reliable confirmation that they are not usurers. But if they do not bring you such confirmation, then tell them that first, you are commanded by God not to regard a usurer as a Christian—and that he himself should not consider himself a Christian under that same command.

92. Second, the emperor also forbade considering a usurer as a just man. Therefore, any usurer should not regard himself as a pious man under that same law. For who are we to want to take away God's and the emperor's rights and reverse their meaning?

93. And aren't you such a miser that you refuse contributing even a dime for my living or to relieve the hardship of a poor man but instead, dear friend, rob and steal from both of them? Well, in that case, I would only condemn myself and not do you any good if I wanted to absolve you because neither God nor the emperor would recognize this as legally valid.

94. Therefore, repent and act righteous! If you don't, you can just as easily go to hell alone, without me and my absolution. For you would go to hell together with me if I gave you absolution—you'd take me with you not through my guilt but through sharing yours. No, my fine friend! You go alone while I stay here! I am not a pastor, so I can accompany anyone into hell but would rather bring everyone to God with me!

* * *

REVIEW QUESTIONS

1. Why is it proper for "princes" (i.e., the authorities) to rip up unconscionable contracts?

2. In the segment "What We Clergymen Need to Do," Luther gives specific instructions to pastors on how to respond to usury and treat confirmed usurers. What does he want them to do?

3. In paragraphs 86 and 87, Luther warns pastors that not withholding sacrament, absolution, and Christian burial from confirmed

usurers endangers their own salvation. Why would pastors suffer from the sins of these usurers?

Study Questions

1. In his Large Catechism, Luther wrote the following under the seventh commandment:

   > Furthermore, at the market and in everyday business the same fraud prevails in full power and force. One person openly cheats another with defective merchandise, false weights and measures, and counterfeit coins, and takes advantage of the other by deception and sharp practices and crafty dealings. . . . This is why these people are also called armchair bandits, and highway-robbers. Far from being pick-locks and sneak-thieves who pilfer the cash box, they sit in their chairs and are known as great lords and honorable, while they rob and steal under the cloak of legality.[9]

   Discuss this connection among shady trade practices in general, the usury at the core of this "Exhortation," and the commandment not to steal.

2. In paragraph 81, Luther laments that usury may already have become unstoppable. Now, Luther is considering interest payments on what we would call "consumer credit"—money spent on the necessities of life. He is not considering "investment credit" used to build new factories or develop new products. In Luther's time, investment credit was largely unknown, except for in the large bank houses, such as the Fugger Banking House in Augsburg. Discuss the difference between these two types of credit.

3. Discuss how Luther's argument would change when applied to a business credit for investment instead of a consumer credit taken out under conditions of duress.

4. In paragraph 82, Luther refers to the capability of many authorities to annul contracts deemed "unfair" by custom. American law knows such contracts as "unconscionable" contracts or

---

9 BC, 417.

clauses, rendered void by legally acknowledging them as such. What anecdotes about surprising effects of credit card debt or student loans have you heard? Provided they are true, discuss them in light of the concept of "unconscionable" contracts.

5. Luther demands pastors treat usurers harshly, since they must be considered, in essence, as outside the Christian community and congregation. Looking at today's circumstance, do you see any groups around policy making or execution of credit or financial services that could possibly deserve or should be exempt from such treatment? Examine the reasons for your views.

* * *

Part VI

Charitable Exception for the Needy

95. But what if there were the case of old people, poor widows, orphans, or other needy persons who never learned any other way to earn a living? Pretend they would have one or two thousand gulden in commerce. Should they now abandon these so as to have nothing left and therefore be reduced to poverty, in danger of starving to death?

96. Here I would much appreciate if the lawyers came up with a mitigation of their strict law! We also need to keep in mind that all the princes and lords mentioned above who opposed usury—like Solon, Alexander, and the Romans—could not or did not want to eliminate it completely. Also, Nehemiah did not restore everything. Perhaps in this situation, the above saying actually does apply: "The world cannot be without usury!"

97. For in the true sense, this exception for the needy would not be genuine usury at all but rather a small usurious act born of calamity, almost like a work of merciful charity for those needy, who otherwise would have nothing. Furthermore, it would not impose undue damage on their neighbors. It could also be argued that this might be a case of *interesse*,[1] or *Schadewacht*, for the needy would experience disadvantage because they failed to learn any other breadwinning skill. Also, it would be quite rude and would not benefit anyone to make these people into beggars or to make them die of hunger, especially since it happens without harming one's neighbor as a result of "uncertain restitution."[2]

---

1 See explanation of this Latin term in footnote 5, p. 33.
2 Latin: *ex restitutione vaga*. A situation where the benefactor of the restitution is unknown or unknowable.

98. But this is not my call to make, although I would like to advise and help so that nobody has to despair in sin. That is why in this matter, I consider it best to call upon the local sovereign to find out, together with reasonable lawyers, preachers, and councilors, a passable solution—fairness or amnesty[3]—suitable to soothe the conscience.

99. As for the rest, I know full well what kind of stinging law one can introduce. But necessity breaks iron! It can therefore probably break a law, especially since necessity and choice[4] are far apart from each other and also play very different roles in terms of time and person. What is right without hardship is wrong—indeed, an injustice, in a case of need, and vice versa. Anyone who takes the baker's bread off the counter without famine is a thief, but if he does so in a famine, he is justified, for we owe him bread. There are many more situations like this. But as I said, he who needs answers to such things may find out from his prince, pastor, and pious scholars. What they advise he better obey! Not everything can be put in writing.

100. Perhaps it may serve or help us knowing that the emperor Justinian limited usury so as to allow the nobles to take four gulden; the merchants, eight; and everyone else, six, on one hundred gulden.[5] And when Justinian said he wanted to lessen the old, hard, heavy burden of usury, this can provide advice in our case as well. I will gladly agree with it and help carry it before God, especially when it concerns needy persons and a usurious act caused by a mishap or if merciful usury should be present.

101. But if it was a wanton, stingy usury not caused by need, directed only at trade and profit, I would not want to vote for it nor give my advice (for lending should not and cannot be a trade, business, or profit) but rather leave that responsibility to the emperor. Do not even care what the emperor's opinion may be. The emperor cannot teach good works, for they belong to heaven. For him, it is sufficient that he teaches good works in this temporal life—just as his words said: he wanted to mollify usury so that the hard and heavy load will be relieved.

102. Therefore, just obeying the emperor's laws is insufficient for heaven. And yet we accept what he gracefully provides—especially when

---

3 Greek: *epieikeia* or *amnestia*.

4 "Choice" in the sense of absence of necessity or distress.

5 That is, nobles got to take 4 percent interest; merchants, 8 percent; and everyone else, 6 percent.

he provides in the form of temporal goods and in times of dire need what is under the control of his government. Besides, now is not the time to expect that charging 5 or 6 percent will make you wealthy. And certainly, it is no time for needy people who cannot lend their received interest back out again because they need to consume it supporting themselves. But beyond that, good advice given in private by pious people may be best. Pastors should refer these people to lawyers or persons of honor[6] and refuse disputing it from the pulpit. Let that suffice for basic instruction.

USURY AMONG THE HEATHEN

103. We can now see what a reprehensible thing usury is, how it devours the world and, before they realize it, carries away even good people so that they know neither in nor out. Therefore, in the end it must be controlled with great force, and utmost wisdom must advise the pious for as long as no sufficient law can be found to ward off this vicious vice. Therefore, Saint Paul says, "But those who want to be rich fall into temptation and are trapped by many senseless and harmful desires that plunge people into ruin and destruction" [1 Tim 6:9]. Surely Paul saw how stinginess and usury in the Roman Empire had plagued the world—and still plagues it. For who can tell how many evil and vile desires and thoughts such a usurer must have to keep his usury fed well? All day and all night he remains nothing but money and stinginess.

104. Why are usurers not content with what God gives them? It says, "But if we have food and clothing, we will be content with these" [1 Tim 6:8]. This is said to all Christians, both rich and poor. The reason, Paul explains, is this: "We brought nothing into the world, so that we can take nothing out of it" [1 Tim 6:7]. A prince has food and clothing according to his person. No more can he personally consume, and everything else he has to leave behind—like any other citizen, farmer, and beggar.

105. But stinginess and usury scrabble, scratch, and gather as if they want to devour everything or carry it out of this world, even though they need no more food and clothing than anyone else. The people's motto remains: "Dressed well and fed well, what is inside me and what clothes me—that is all I need before I die!" Anything beyond that, men may have along with God as did David and the rich people, yet others can

---

6 Latin: *bonos viros*.

share to use it with him. For himself, he has nothing more but food and clothing—like any other man.

106. Even if his food and clothing are more precious, they still are no more than food and clothing. For his house and castle, his country and his garb—they are his "clothing"; likewise, his food and drink, his wine and beer are considered nothing but his "food." And "food" here does not mean fodder for animals; neither does "clothing" just mean any rag or sackcloth. Rather, "food and clothing" are the fulfillment of a need each of us has for all the goods according to his walk of life.[7] If this were not the case, then all men would have to eat hay and straw, even the princes and lords, for we Christians were told that all of us—one no different from another—cannot use goods beyond what we need for food and clothing. We all should be content with that, though food and clothing must remain different according to the differences among individuals.

107. Thereby and in a worldly manner, enough is said about the restraint and the combating of usury by the heathen. As said above, in modest cases they allowed—or more precisely, tolerated—usury.

108. The heathen let usury go unpunished to avoid even greater evils. This is no different from many other things that remained tolerated and unpunished among them, which Christ does not allow and we, therefore, cannot accept among us—such as envy and treachery, cunning and malice. Moses, too, still permitted divorce and many things that Christ would not allow his Christians. For secular law governs the earthly, mortal, and fluctuating kingdom, but Christ's righteousness rules the heavenly, eternal, and consistent kingdom [Matt 5:31].

109. That is why his scepter is also called "a straight scepter"[8] [Ps 45:6]. This is a very pure and perfect law, a law without fault, lack, crookedness, patches, or wrinkles. Since his law can tolerate neither usury nor evil at all, there certainly can be no usury if one only keeps that law and is a Christian: as little as a Christian is a heathen or a Jew, so little, then, is he a usurer.

* * *

---

7 "His walk of life" could also be translated more literally as "his status and office."

8 In the tract, Luther used the Latin, *sceptrum rectitudinis*, which he translated as "gerades Zepter"—"straight scepter"—in his German Bible of 1545. Modern translations usually translate this phrase as "right," or "righteous scepter," or as "scepter of justice."

REVIEW QUESTIONS

1. Beginning in paragraph 95, Luther proposes an exception for his
    general message on usury. What is it, and why is it prudent in
    Luther's view?
2. Luther argues for a concept of "enough," in the sense of "suffi-
    cient," when it comes to material possessions. What reasoning
    does he propose? What biblical references does he quote?
3. Following the "laws of the emperor" is sufficient for heathen.
    What does Luther demand of Christian behavior?

STUDY QUESTIONS

1. In paragraph 99, Luther explains that someone grabbing a loaf
    of bread from the baker's counter during a famine is justified in
    his action, for "we owe him bread." The biblical reference for this
    is Deuteronomy 23:25. What do you think of this statement?
2. Until 1975, German law had a special clause called *Mundraub*
    (literally, theft by or right into the mouth) to impose lighter sen-
    tences for food theft in situations of desperate need. Find out if
    your jurisdiction has such an exemption. Discuss the merits of
    handling this situation differently from petty theft.
3. In paragraphs 105 and 106, Luther discusses the idea that per-
    sonal consumption for a given person has natural limits: food
    can be luxurious, but there is still only so much of it that any one
    of us can eat. Discuss how this may apply to other goods. How
    many Porsches, houses, private jets, and so on does a wealthy
    person "need" in Luther's sense? Why do others not care to own
    beyond their actual needs?
4. In paragraph 106, Luther explains that "'food' here does not
    mean fodder for animals; neither does 'clothing' just mean any
    rag or sackcloth." Discuss this idea with respect to contemporary
    "transfer payments" from "the rich" in support of "the poor":
    How would you measure that material assistance is sufficient for
    supporting the poor?
5. Some Scandinavian countries have a progressive taxation in
    which personal annual income beyond a certain threshold is
    almost entirely taxed away. In the light of his writing on the
    limits of personal consumption, discuss what Luther might have

to say about this. What if individuals were to use their private property in excess of personal consumption to invest into new economic endeavors?

6. Historically, the United States' top federal tax bracket in 1953, under President Eisenhower, was 91 (ninety-one!) percent for incomes over $400,000. Beginning with the Reagan administration, substantial cuts were enacted, most recently in 2017. Today's rate is about 37 percent for incomes over about $629,000. Would raising the tax bracket percentage for higher incomes work in today's United States? Why or why not? How have US federal finances performed since Eisenhower?

* * *

Part VII

How Christians Should Give

110. That is his law, and accordingly, he taught his Christians the three ways to deal with temporal goods. We have often talked about that, and it is written clearly in Matthew and Luke. [See Matt 5:20–44 and Luke 6:30–35.]

111. First, Christians should give willingly: "You should give to anyone who asks you."[1] But whoever gives evidently does not exercise usury because he donates it for free and desires nothing in return. That is why among Christians there cannot be any usurers.

112. Second, they should like to lend out or be borrowed from. Of this, Christ speaks in Luke: "But love your enemies, do good, and lend, expecting nothing in return" [Luke 6:35].[2] Whoever shares in this way will certainly not commit usury.

113. Third, a Christian should accept that the coat be taken together with the shirt. As he explains himself in Matthew, this includes the suffering of all kinds of injustice and violence. He says, "If anyone forces you to go one mile, go also the second mile. . . . Love your enemies and pray for those who persecute you" [Matt 5:41, 44]. Whoever now observes this and behaves this way—how can he act usuriously? Such a Christian does not act usuriously with others, but he secures his advantage[3] with God! But more on that later.

---

1 Latin: *omni petenti te tribue*. See Luke 6:30.

2 WA gives Luke 6:34 as, in Latin, *Mutuum dantes* and so on; more likely seems a reference to 6:35, saying in Latin, *Benefacite, et mutuum date, nihil inde sperantes*—that is, "Do good, and lend, expecting nothing in return."

3 More literally, "exercises wonderful usury" with God. In a footnote, WA suggests the translation used above.

COMMON OBJECTIONS

114. Here you say, "Well, shall anyone now be a Christian who wants to and is able to?" The answer is that whoever wants to become saved in the kingdom of heaven may as well be a Christian. Now you ask, "Who can be saved, anyway?" Anyone who wants to be a Christian can very well have salvation. Christ will not align, bend, turn, or steer his word to conform to us. For it is said, "Your Empire's scepter is a straight, equal and upright scepter!" [Heb 1:8; see also Ps 47:6].[4] That is just how it is. Therefore, it is us who have to align and conform. A cubit is not measured by the cloth but the cloth by the cubit or else measuring means nothing at all! The weight must not be weighed by the goods, but the goods by weight. What else would be weighing?

115. That was hard and unbearable for the Sophists and papists and also for Mohammed.[5] That is why they came up with something easier and better. They teach, therefore, that Christ would have commanded such rules not to all Christians but only to those who were perfect. Everyone else remains free whether he wishes to keep such rules or not. Namely, anyone wanting to earn more and higher rewards than eternal salvation, he may abide by them. But if he is satisfied already and does not desire anything more than just to be saved, he may ignore these rules and is not obligated to follow them.

116. In this way, they[6] have made such fine Christians of us that we finally have to buy surplus merit from the saints, even from the priests and monks. That means they turned us into wholesome pagans and Turks, indeed even worse than heathen and Turks. They accuse us[7] of forbidding good works. But let us look at the text at hand, and it will become clear who really forbids good works! For in fact, they are the ones who not only prohibit good works but even remove the teaching of Christ by which he commands good works. And they declare that one must neither hold such doctrines nor do such good works.

117. Dear friend, what is left for good works if the doctrine of the good works is prohibited, condemned, and destroyed? What is left of

---

4 Latin: *virga aequitatis, virga regni tui.* WA references Ps 47:7 but more likely seems Ps 45:6. On the translation as "straight scepter," see also part VI, footnote 8.
5 A reference to the founder of Islam.
6 That is, the pope and the Catholic clergy.
7 That is, Luther himself and his teachings.

them except for what we chose to do, acting without and against God's commands just like the Turks, Tatars,[8] and Jews? It is for this reason that the world is full of monks, cowls, and masses but without genuine Christians and without such good works as giving, lending, and suffering. But we,[9] who on our part teach such good deeds and demand them in accordance with the words of Christ, are presented as those who forbid good works.

118. They make for fine saints indeed, those who not only condemn the doctrine of the good works to prevent all good works but also claim everywhere that it is us who forbid the good works, even though we teach such good works against their damnation and prohibition. So their own heretical and devilish teachings are what they charge us with, and our own Christian teachings these fine bigots claim as their own.

119. Then you say, "Well, how can I possibly give something to everyone? As they say, it would take a rich merchant to do such a thing. Even the emperor finds it impossible to give to everyone. This is possible only for God but not some human being." I have preached and written about this often enough—and so have others with me. No one would need our interpretation, and everyone could see it our way, if only they were to study this text diligently. But since none of us is sufficiently diligent, we are required to direct one another through this text by pointing with our fingers so that the other person also sees it and not merely takes our word for it but rather examines himself and understands the Lord's Word.

120. First, when our Lord says that you should give to everyone [Matt 5:42], then here, "everyone" does not mean that I should give to each and every person on earth or to all the needy in the world. God knows well that this would be impossible. Rather, he referred to that text describing the Jewish conception of the law that said, "You shall love your friend and hate your enemy!" [Matt 5:43; Lev 19:18]. From this, the Jews concluded and taught that one would have to give not to everyone but only to friends, because one should love only the friends but hate the enemies.

121. Against this, Christ speaks: you shall do unto every man—that is, not only your friend but also your enemy. And exclude no one—be it enemy or friend—in his trouble and hardship. His words are quite clear

---

8 *Tatars* is a contemporary term for Mongols who invaded parts of Europe in the thirteenth century.

9 That is, Luther himself and his teachings. See, for example, Luther's treatise *On Good Works*, LW 44:15–114.

when he says, "For if you love those who love you, what reward do you have? Do not even the tax collectors do the same?" [Matt 5:46–47].

122. This is also the way of the world, expressed by saying, "Look over the fence and I'll do the same for you!"[10] But if my neighbor just wants to say to me, "Dear friend, look over the fence—that is, see how I feel, help and advise me, be a good neighbor," and if he does not want to hear me reply, "You too better also look back and are a good neighbor," then the world's friendship comes to an end. For such worldly friendship does not look over the fence if no one wants to look back in return. The Greeks expressed this by saying, "One hand washes the other."

123. But as Christ teaches here, a Christian should always look over the fence for the neighbor's need and to help, even if his neighbor never looks back. For God will compensate with an overabundant look on his part. This is why Saint Paul in Romans also cites Solomon's saying: "If your enemies are hungry, feed them; if they are thirsty, give them something to drink" [Rom 12:20]. Even Moses speaks: "When you see the donkey of one who hates you lying under its burden and you would hold back from setting it free, you must help to set it free" [Exod 23:5].

124. Second, "everyone" does not mean someone who already has or can get enough because it is—especially at this time—evil rogues who pose as poor, needy, and destitute, trying to deceive the people. If the authorities were not so negligent and lazy and the gallows were not so vainly put on the street as if they were on holiday, then one should have alms administered to such people from the executioner in the form of rope and sack.

125. That is why there are so many loiterers here who are lively, healthy, and strong, that are well capable to work, serve, and support themselves. But they prefer to rely on Christians and pious people happy to provide for them. And if this giving is not rich or good enough in their eyes, they supplement it by stealing, even by bold public grabbing on the farms, in the streets, and inside houses. I do not know if there has ever been such a time when stealing and taking were so commonplace. And yet all these gallows stand completely idle, observing holidays for years.

126. Christ has not demanded such giving here! Only the needy in your city and surroundings should be given to. As Moses teaches, one should only help, give, lend to those—be it friends or foes—who cannot work, serve, and feed themselves or whose faithful work and services

---

10 Literally, "Look over the fence and back again."

prove insufficient for self-support [Deut 15:11]. Any Christian can do likewise! It is not even difficult for him where rulers bar foreign beggars and vagrants as well as strange and lazy people from their lands.[11]

127. Third, a Christian, before he can donate anything, of course, must first own something—he who owns nothing cannot possibly donate anything! And if he is to give again tomorrow, the day after tomorrow, and throughout the year (because Christ commands me to donate as long as I live), then he cannot possibly give everything away today. So when the Lord Christ commands us to give, he openly commands it only to those who own something and are thus able to donate. Otherwise, it would mean to search where nothing can be found.

128. Incidentally, the monks have masterfully avoided this commandment. While some of them have had nothing to give away when they became monks, they were looking for something from the monastery—or more precisely from its kitchen—just to fill their bellies. However, it is true that some of them gave away all they had. But all of them receive something in return—forever. All received and accepted gifts eternally until they got more in return than the entire world possessed. Indeed, this is a fine way to give—namely, giving a penny in return for a thousand gulden.

129. This is also very unoriginal. Against this, Saint Paul already taught the Corinthians that he did not expect of them that they give in such a way "that there should be relief for others and pressure on you" [2 Cor 8:13],[12] that they suffer while those to whom they give are enjoying a good time. No, our Lord Christ does not expect that! He does not want me to become a beggar of my own making by converting beggars into lords!

130. I am only supposed to take care of his need and help him within my abilities! The poor person should join me at my table to eat, not I join him at his. But I ought not to take from my family's needs to give to others! This a Christian may well do, even to his enemy—though a Jew or pagan would certainly not do this to his enemy. So that is the

---

11 A reference to legislation in many Lutheran lands and cities that established what we would call government-run social services, including welfare handouts from the "common chest" for the—registered and officially acknowledged—poor in their places. See, for example, Lindberg and Wee, *Forgotten Luther*; and Carter Lindberg, *Beyond Charity: Reformation Initiatives for the Poor* (Minneapolis: Fortress, 1993).

12 Latin: *ut aliis remissio, ipsis tribulatio sit.*

true meaning of "give to anyone who asks you"! Asking is not allowed for those without need; if they ask anyway, they would have to be rascals.

131. But being in need is something entirely different. At times, some people need very much, indeed above and beyond all measure, to serve their useless and shameful splendor and pride. May the devil provide enough to them! Christ, however, is in conversation with his Christians who are called to suffer with him. Preparing for eternal life, they use life in this world, each one according to their walk of life.[13] He says, "You should not fly high!" [Luke 12:29].[14]

132. Who can give, lend, or have taken from him enough to satisfy the squandering and all the wanton pride and splendor of a pope, cardinal, bishop, prince, lord, nobleman, citizen, and peasant? We should all have enough if it suffices for the needs of the body,[15] and no one shall let their neighbor linger in trouble, not even their enemy! Thus, Saint Paul speaks in his first letter to Timothy, "But if we have food and clothing, we will be content with these" [1 Tim 6:8].

* * *

Review Questions

1. Luther presents the three ways in which Christians can give without committing usury. Identify them.

2. In paragraph 114, Luther says, "A cubit is not measured by the cloth but the cloth by the cubit" when the Word is measuring us and our deeds. What does he mean by that?

3. In paragraph 116, Luther mocks that we now have to "buy surplus merit from the saints, even from the priests and monks." What is he referring to?

4. Luther describes a case of medieval "fake news." What does he say?

---

13 "Walk of life" could also be translated more literally as "status and office."

14 Luther paraphrases from Luke 12:29 in his translation of 1545: "Darum auch ihr, fraget nicht darnach, was ihr essen oder was ihr trinken sollt, und fahret nicht hoch her"—Thus do not ask what you shall eat or drink, and you shall not fly high (WA DB 6:270–71).

15 Latin: *habentes victum.*

5. In paragraphs 124 and 125, Luther describes what is called the "undeserving poor," as distinguished from the genuinely needy. What behaviors is he describing?

6. Luther explains that in order for a Christian to "give," he first must "have." What does he mean?

STUDY QUESTIONS

1. In paragraph 115, Luther introduces the idea to distinguish "perfect" Christians from other Christians who have somewhat lesser aspirations. He reports that some traditions teach that following all the rules is only meant for the "perfect" Christians, and everyone else gets to decide on their own. Discuss this idea of "perfect" Christians as a group held to a higher standard within Christianity. Where this idea is followed among Christians, what practical consequences would you expect?

2. The second objection Luther refutes is that no one can give to "everyone." Describe his defense. What shapes does this argument take today?

3. Beginning in paragraph 127, Luther explains the idea of lifelong, sustainable giving. What would this look like for us moderns? What role does government play in this context?

4. In paragraph 132, Luther criticizes the establishment of his time for consuming more than its share and not giving in accordance with its wealth. In your opinion, how is the contemporary establishment doing in this respect?

* * *

Part VIII

Giving with Sincerity

133. On top of all this, there is one more thing to note on giving so as to not turn it into roguishness. It concerns not the outward hand, the wallet, or the chest,[1] but the heart. The Lord says about this in Matthew, "But when you give alms, do not let your left hand know what your right hand is doing" [Matt 6:3]. This and similar matters we have covered diligently before, but here we need to consider this a little closer still.

134. For what has been said thus far is still insufficient: that you give both to friends and enemies but, above all, to the needy; and that you still retain enough so you and yours have enough to eat; and also that you retain enough to donate again next time for as long as you live. In addition and above all, see to it that giving follows Saint Paul's teaching in Romans: "If anyone gives, let him do it with sincerity"[2] [Rom 12:8 NMB]. That is, give with a sincere heart and not for the sake of honor. Likewise, the giver shall do what he can to quickly forget his deed and return to a state as if he had never given anything or done any good!

135. For otherwise, the devil will happily fasten his rope on the deed. Then one takes pride in giving and wants to be seen in the process; these are the people that have trumpet sounds herald them. Of these, Christ says in Matthew that they like to hear said about them, "See how well gives such-and-such; God help him, or else he'll donate himself to death."[3]

---

1   This refers to the "common chest" Luther and his fellow reformers had introduced in many cities. From the "common chest," the authorities distributed monetary relief to the recognized poor in their midst. See also footnote 11, p. 69.

2   Most English translations interpret this phrase as "the giver should be generous or give with 'simplicity.'" The translation given here is from the New Matthew Bible and better reflects Luther's original wording.

3   The WA references Matt 6 here.

These people have gambled away their reward because such giving is completely lost and in vain!

136. But even more annoying are those who give with the intent to bind those to whom they give something. They seek their own advantage in an exceptionally shameful manner. They want you to celebrate them, to accept them and let them talk; they want you to suffer and let happen and serve whatever and however they please. Meanwhile, you cannot hope to ever thank them enough.

137. All this is just as if I were giving ten gulden to a needy person in his distress to please him with it. But then go on to use and exploit him, making him serve me more than even a hundred gulden would buy me from my servant or from my maid to whom I would otherwise owe pay for their work and service. Such giving—done only in the hope of being able to buy something much cheaper than elsewhere or to save on wages—you and I would probably also dislike.

Incidentally, this is exactly the same way in which quite a few noblemen but also towns and villages play on their pastors, although they have neither donated the parishes nor contributed anything to them. Because they have the power to assign the parish, they simply want to make pastors into their slaves. But they themselves refuse to endure the same treatment. For if the princes—from whom, in turn, they received their fiefdoms—would follow suit, they would want to make them slaves or tell them what the prince desires them to do.

138. In this way, they want the pastor to do whatever they please as an expression of gratitude, while at the same time, they only want to suffer from their own overlord what they choose, although they ought to be just as thankful to their lords as the pastor is to them. Now, you tell me, what kind of giving is this? It is, as stated above, a penny for a thousand gulden. This is indeed buying cheaply—dear friend, teach me that trick! And yet, they want to have the glory of being called benefactors, not takers; they want to be called Christians and desire to be saved.

139. From this, you can see that any giving that, as was said above, refers only to hand or wallet is indeed not difficult—be it donating to friend or to foe. But giving from the heart without any agenda—that is hard! When measured this way, few turn out to be actual Christians! And yet it is not difficult; it costs neither money nor work. It only requires sending forth the heart in the right way. He who gives a single penny with an unassuming heart gives more before God than if he had given a hundred or even a hundred thousand gulden with a

false heart because God does not consider that a gift! Now, where does this leave these wannabe noblemen[4] and those especially fine brothers[5] who now are merely veritable takers but nonetheless want to be called givers?

140. I have often observed with great aversion how princes, lords, nobles, citizens, and peasants shamefully squander so much through pride, splurging, gambling, and so on. They could certainly help many needy people if they only could bring themselves to donate the tenth or even the hundredth part of what they waste. But I have consoled myself and reasoned that even if they would give to the poor, they would do so only from a false heart. That is why it is a lot better if they spend a thousand gulden in the devil's name than if they were donating a penny in God's name! Before God, they are not worthy to contribute the value of even one brass farthing to God's service and honor! For those who spend a thousand gulden in the devil's name at least cannot boast they have given anything for God's sake or to the poor. They can extract from it neither any compulsory services nor any services at all, like the false benefactors do. They only condemn themselves.

141. But those who give such false gulden in the name of God so much want to defy and out-dare God, requesting much gratitude and so many services in return. Not only is Mammon their god, but through their Mammon, they themselves now want to be god to the world and fancy to be worshipped accordingly. But yet the poor, though they neither can nor want to have Mammon for their god, are now supposed to worship Mammon's divinity as represented by its idols—I should rather say, by its gods—or die of hunger. Reason tells us such giving is not to give but to take sevenfold.

142. Sirach therefore calls them fools—that is, godless people. In chapter 20, he says, "A fool's gift will profit you nothing, for he looks for recompense sevenfold" [Sir 20:14].[6]

---

4 German: *junkerlein*.
5 With intended irony, Luther literally writes, "golden brothers."
6 This translation relays the meaning well. However, Luther quotes this verse as the "fool giving with one (sincere) eye, while with seven eyes, seeing what he gets in return" (*Mit einem Auge gibt er, und mit sieben Augen sieht er, was er dafür bekommt*). For more on the book of Sirach, see "A Few Words on Formatting and Translation" on p. 14.

As you continue reading there, Sirach describes such nefarious people that complain, for example, that they receive insufficient gratitude for their good deeds or in return for the bread one was allowed to taste from their hands. They are almost of the kind described in the song of Saint Martin: "Dearest Sir Saint Martin, what are you looking for among the great thieves? They donate a penny on your behalf and steal your horse. They are such big thieves that they'll probably hang one day."

143. In this sense, I am afraid, many of the monasteries and cloisters were built for this very reason, and many masses and church services were set up only to buy from God his kingdom with evil and that false coin called "our own work and merit." But God will burn them with infernal fire just as you would burn counterfeit coins!

LENDING WITH SINCERITY

144. We also need to talk about lending in the same spirit that we talked about borrowing. First, a Christian should lend not only to his friends but also to his enemies. The Lord says, "For if you love those who love you, what reward do you have? Do not even the tax collectors do the same?" [Matt 5:46; see also Luke 6:34].

145. Second is that you lend to the needy and not to the rogues, to the lazy, or to them that splurge, as has already been said above about giving. Sirach explains, "Many regard a loan as a windfall" [Sir 29:4], with no intention to pay it back. Such lazy rogues abuse Christ's commandment; they rely on us being obligated to lend to them. So you should not lend them anything.

146. Third is that one only lends when one actually has something to lend and then lends only in such a way that he can lend again tomorrow or next year. Otherwise, the saying is true: "If you do not give it back to me, then I cannot lend it to you anymore." This means I would have to end my lending, since I have nothing more to lend. This is what Sirach means when he says in chapter 29 that some people refuse to lend because they fear losing what is theirs [Sir 29:7].

147. By the way, you can completely copy that chapter from Sirach in here. It explains to you very nicely how things usually go with lending. For even in times long gone, this saying went around in schools: if you have lent something to somebody, you will not get it back; if you get it back, you will not get it back quickly; if you get it back quickly, you will

not get it back in as good a condition; if you get it back in as good a condition, you lose the friend![7]

148. On the other hand, however, the children of Adam are very
bitter when they are instructed to lend even the tiniest thing to one who
offended them. To such a person, they wish every evil thing and throw
every curse known to the mercenaries. Yet they want to be Christians and
receive the sacrament. Therefore, everyone needs to find out for themselves and according to their conscience when, where, how much, and to
whom they should give or are obliged to lend or give! No other yardsticks
can be set here than the need of the neighbor and Christian love. God
has commanded us to show our neighbors the love of Christ in the same
way we want to experience it through others—no matter if we are friends
or enemies.

149. Such lending is neither difficult nor impossible. Therefore, not
even the sophists had reason to change our Lord's commandment into
suggestions—what they call advice.[8] Even reason teaches us that one
should do to the other what he wants the other to do to him. The Lord
himself says, "In everything do to others as you would have them do to
you" [Matt 7:12]. This is what the law and all the prophets rule. Indeed,
all natural laws say the same thing here.

150. However, I most certainly would like to be given to, lent to,
and helped in times of need. On the other hand, it is just as certain that
nobody should give, lend, or help me when I do not need it; when I am
lazy or a rascal; if I only want to splurge but not work; if I do not want to
achieve or endure anything, even though I am perfectly able to, healthy
and strong. In this case, I would not lack anything if people acting too
piously provided sufficiently for me—even though they should afterward
justly have me whipped, chased out of the country, or hanged on the
gallows.

151. As I have said above of giving, it is a heavy and rare way of lending with a sincere heart, without any agenda, without asking anything in
return, and without coercing my neighbor or making him into my bond-
slave. I am not speaking here of usurious lending, as above, but of lending, without usury, to enemies and friends alike—that is, lending as far
away from outward works as one can get. As donors want to be celebrated

---

7 Latin: *si commodaveris, non rehabebis; si rehabehis, non tam cito; si tam cito, non
tam bonum; si tam bonum, perdes amicum!*

8 Latin: *consilia.* See paragraph 115 for the sophists' suggestion.

and worshipped by those who receive from them, those lending out often want to be celebrated by those who have to borrow from them. That is why Christian lending is as rare as Christian giving. The seven eyes, as Sirach says, still leave the one sincere eye blind [Sir 20:14].[9]

BEING ANOTHER'S GOD

152. All in all, the misery and heartache of one man desiring to be another's god are caused by that apple in Paradise, where even Adam and Eve wanted to be gods in the name of the devil. Each one of us still carries that same apple in our belly: time and again it belches out of us while refusing to be ever quite fully digested. Even the true saints have something of it still within them—at least some of that apple's core.

153. We see from this how quite a few people can rejoice when other people are suffering. This applies especially to the idolaters, as Saint Paul calls the miserly and usurious [Eph 5:5]. They relish it if you cannot get by without their services, require their help, and have to appeal to them—don't we know them all?

154. Just look at those holding back the grain: how they hope and how happy they become when its price increases, how sad they become when grain becomes cheap. Also consider the many usurers and pinchpennies who hang themselves over this: God regards all usurers worthy of the same justice and judgment. Incidentally, it would be a real pity if they were to be hanged by public hangmen in a legal and honest manner. Instead, let them just be their own shameful executioners and shamefully hang themselves, acting as their very own devils and deaths—just as they liked acting as the world's murderers and robbers.

155. Contrary to this, Christ our Lord has commanded no one should desire to be another's god; instead, in their love, everyone should be a servant to their neighbor! No one should wish or hope for the other's misfortune, nor enjoy it! Everyone should be compassionate and gracious toward his neighbor's need and misfortune! Christ himself has given us a unique example, of which Saint Paul writes in his letter to the Philippians: "Who, though he was in the form of God, did not regard equality with God as something to be exploited, but emptied himself, taking the form of a slave" [Phil 2:6–7].

* * *

9 See footnote 6, p. 75.

REVIEW QUESTIONS

1. What does Luther mean by someone giving "with sincerity"?
2. Beginning in paragraph 136, Luther develops the ill-intended side of "giving." What does he point out? Where do you see this leading?
3. How would you summarize the effects of giving with a "false heart"?
4. In the final analysis, what does the donation with "false coin" amount to? It is yet another manifestation of a mistake whose correction is central to Luther's teaching. What is the mistake?
5. At the close of paragraph 147, Luther quotes an old Latin saying describing the way lending often goes. How does this reflect your own experiences with lending? Consider especially lending within your family.
6. In a rather enjoyable phrase, Luther blames the proverbial apple of Genesis for usurious behavior and its consequences. What is he saying?

STUDY QUESTIONS

1. The Anglo-Saxon world, in particular, has the habit of ostensibly celebrating philanthropist donors. It is customary to permanently attach their names to the libraries, hospital wings, professorships, and art collections they gave. In the light of Luther's mandate to give with "sincerity," how would he look at this practice?
2. Moses Maimonides (1135–1204 CE) was one of the great Jewish thinkers. Go online and find a copy of Maimonides's "Eight Levels of Charity" or "Tzedakah." For example, see https://www.jewishvirtuallibrary.org/what-is-tzedakah. Discuss how the thinking of Luther and Maimonides compare.
3. In paragraph 138, Luther discusses the example of citizens influencing who gets to be pastor in a given parish by those who make the call. Discuss today's concept of corporate (not private) "campaign donations" with respect to this idea of "giving." Can you see any parallels? Why or why not?
4. In paragraph 141, Luther gets to the core problem that "love of money" creates. In violation of the first commandment, usurers

put Mammon in the place of God. Where do you recognize this today? What examples can you find where individuals, groups, or institutions seem to adhere to a "religion of money"—that is, they let the needs of money dominate all other considerations in their decision-making?

5. In paragraph 152, Luther observes that usurers aggravate their violation of the first commandment by seeing themselves as fellow deities, deserving and demanding worship from those depending on the credit they offer. Where do you recognize such behavior today?

* * *

Part IX

Usurers Come after Their Father, the Devil

156. By contrast, avaricious people usuriously extract, stingily swipe, conquer, and steal to create their divinity and establish dominion over the poor and needy. They enjoy and lust at the fact that they are rich through money and others are poor; that they reign through their money; that others must worship them.

157. In this respect, they follow only their father, the devil. While in heaven, he also attempted to usuriously acquire divinity and scrooge it together with the angelical riches, ornament, and glory bestowed on him and placing him above all angels. But he fell and lost both—the usurious gain and the principal sum. In this way, he was converted from the most beautiful image of God into God's most hideous enemy.

158. Therefore, after the devil himself, there is, on earth, no greater enemy of men than a penny-pinching miser and usurer because he intends to be god above his fellow neighbors. Turks, warriors, and tyrants are also evil persons. But they have to let people live and acknowledge that they are evil and enemies. However, they can—and indeed, they have to, occasionally—take pity on some people. But a usurer and penny-pinching miser-belly with all his strength wants nothing else than seeing all the world perish in hunger and thirst, misery and distress. In this way, he then has everything for himself, and all others can receive from him alone—just as from a god whose eternal slaves they are. Then his heart jumps for joy; this refreshes his blood.

Usurers Try Acting the Innocent

159. All the while, he wants to appear in the splendor of the noblemen, complete with golden necklaces, rings, and robes, yet act the innocent all along. He wants to be seen as a faithful and pious man and praised as such; he wants to be seen as a man who is more merciful than even God himself and friendlier than even the Holy Mother of God and all the saints. And all this he accomplishes (oh, isn't this world tormented?)[1] with a thousand, with a hundred, with fifty gulden or—if the poor man to whom he lends is of a lesser standing—with just a single gulden.

160. From the very beginning and at all times, many wise men have documented very clearly and shown, by means of many horrible examples, how suddenly and awfully usurers perished. Across all languages, there are many proverbs about this: "For what is idly got is idly spent"[2]; "Misappropriated wealth miserably perishes, unjustly strived-for causes are badly ruined. The third heir will not get to enjoy what is wrongly acquired";[3] and as Saint Jerome says, "Every rich man is either unjust or heir to unjustly acquired property."[4] Every day, one can still observe plenty of examples—examples to see, grasp, taste, smell, hear; in short, cases to recognize with all senses. These examples show that goods acquired wrongfully neither prosper nor bequeath. They show that never has a wrongfully acquired good arrived in the third generation. Scripture also confirms this with proud thunder and hellish fire. It says that God, as stated in the first commandment, will exterminate the idol worshippers until the third and fourth generation [Exod 20:5].

161. But without paying heed to all this, the idolaters, usurers, and penny-pinching misers proceed. Blind, hidden, insane, mad, foolish,

---

1 A footnote in WA suggests this to be an ironic remark.
2 Latin: *male partum, male disperit, male quaesit, male perdit.* Attributed to T. Maccius Plavtus (born ca. 254 BCE) in Maccius Plautus, *Poenulus* 4.2.483–844, http://www.thelatinlibrary.com/plautus/poenulus.shtml.
3 Latin: *de male quaesitis non gaudet tertius heres.* This saying is documented in Karl Friedrich Wilhelm Wander, ed., *Deutsches Sprichwörter-Lexikon—Zweiter Band—Gott bis Lehren* (Kettwig: Akademische Verlagsgesellschaft Athenaion, 1867), s.v. "gut," no. 291, col. 199, http://archive.org/details/deutsches-sprichworter-lexikon-band-2-gott-bis-lehren.
4 Luther quotes, "Omnis dives aut iniquus aut heres iniqui." See Sophronius Eusebius Hieronymus and Morin Germain, *Anecdota Maredsolana* vol. 3, part 1 (Maredsous, Belgium: Monasterio S. Benedicti, 1895), http://archive.org/details/commentarioliinoomorigoog. See especially commentary on Ps 83, p. 86.

obsessed, and frantic, they deliberately act against it. So sweet is the poison of that apple in Paradise that they have Mammon as their god and, by his power, want to promote themselves to gods over poor, ruined, and miserable people—not to help or save them but only to aggravate their desolation.

Suggestions for Teaching the People

162. However, since secular rule is negligent and lazy, in this respect, and partly too weak to ward off such misery, pastors should teach the people and train them. First, teach them to consider usurers and misers as bodily devils and to make the sign of the cross on themselves wherever they hear or see them. Second, they are to teach the people to recognize that Turks, Tatars, and other heathen, measured against a usurer, are like genuine angels. Similarly, schoolmasters should teach boys and youth to become frightened and say "Shame on you!" to anyone called a usurer—just like they already do for the worst of devils.

163. Preachers, you can also employ many beautiful fables in which heathen complained of greed and usury. You may recall that Cerberus, the hellhound, has three mouths that can never be fed enough. You can also apply what the heathen tell us about the great deeds of Hercules, who is known to have conquered so many ghastly monsters to save land and people.

164. Every usurer is such a big monster! He is like a werewolf who devastates everything, even worse than any Cacus, Geryon, or Antaeus, which Hercules conquered. Furthermore, he dresses himself up and acts the pious so that one should not see where the oxen went, which he had pulled into his hole—backward.

165. But Hercules is said to have heard the cries of the oxen and the prisoners, the same cries that are now so pitifully appealing to all rulers and lords, and he went to find Cacus, even in the cliffs and rocks, and release the oxen from that villain! For Cacus we call every villain who is a pious usurer, who steals, robs, and devours everything but claims to not have done any of it. Like that Cacus, he wants no one to find out and drags his oxen into the hole backward so that their footsteps create the appearance as if they were not dragged into but rather emerged from the hole. Likewise, usurers want to fool the entire world: Cacus wants to pretend that he serves the world by giving her oxen, when in reality, he steals and devours them.

166. Third, the Lord teaches his Christians to suffer and endure whenever someone takes away what is theirs [Matt 5:38–42]. Since they are not allowed to resist and are not allowed to take personal revenge, it follows that they cannot take back what was violently and wrongly taken from them. They thus must suffer it, especially for the sake of Christ and the gospel. From this, we can now recognize how the dear saints were to become martyrs and endure everything from the heathen; they were to lose everything—including body and life—instead of ever denying Christ or allowing him to be taken from them.

BEWARE OF THE FALSE MARTYRS

167. You ask, "But how about if some people did not suffer at all or did not let anything be taken? Like, if some of them did not suffer with a humble heart but instead pursued honor and glory, as the false benefactors and lenders do?" You need not ask, really. Of course, there were plenty of false martyrs, such as the Manicheans, the Arians, the Donatists, or the Pelagians. Saint Augustine writes of the Donatists that they prize, above all, their great endurance and suffering. Like a poison, so to speak, Satan's wickedness has penetrated into Adam's children so deeply that not only giving and borrowing and all good works but also suffering and endurance can turn a man to error.

168. He can make suffering and endurance far more wrong than good works, for no man is more obdurate, arrogant, and stubborn than a false martyr. He knows how to boast just how large, tall, long, deep, far, and wide he must suffer and bear the cross—and all that supposedly for God's sake. For after hearing that suffering is such a great and glorious thing before God and that Christ praised it most highly [Matt 5:10], they invented their own causes and instantly wanted to be like the genuine holy martyrs.

169. Likewise, even now in our time, the agitators,[5] Anabaptists, and the like are the most stubborn. They instantly consider themselves fine

---

5 German: *rottengeister*. It is possible that Luther here refers to his former fellow reformers Andreas Karlstadt (1486–1541) and Thomas Müntzer (ca. 1490–1525) as well as Huldrych Zwingli (1484–1531) and other Protestants whose teachings he considered rogue and deviant. In his last conversation with Philip Melanchthon, Luther called them "Schwärmer und Rottengeister"—dreamers and agitators. See Th. Diestelmann, *Die letzte Unterredung Luthers mit Melanchthon über den Abendmahlsstreit* (Göttingen: Vandenhoeck & Ruprecht, 1874), 138.

martyrs the moment their ranting and raving is disallowed. A barefoot friar[6] should be refused his fanatical will. He makes such a great holy martyr out of himself that he would not even want to trade his suffering for that of Saint Paul. And so it is that at all times the world is full of martyrs. But most of them are in hell and miss out on heaven.

170. As they go, false martyrs look solely at suffering or endurance, if one can even call that endurance. They do not ask if the suffering is with an unassuming or out of a humble heart. Validity and cause of the suffering they do not care for, although Christ in Matthew explains very clearly: "Blessed are those who suffer for righteousness' sake, or for my sake"[7] [Matt 5:10]. He does not say, "Blessed are those who suffer because of their wickedness, or because of their stubbornness, for the sake of their honor, their avarice, or their glory, their false piety, or for the sake of their self-chosen spirituality."

171. From the outset the cause you suffer for shall be genuine and just! Saint Augustine also often says this fine saying: "Not the suffering but the right cause of suffering makes martyrs!"[8] If this were not so, then the devil and all the damned, all the thieves, murderers, rogues, and other evil people would be greater martyrs than all the saints. It is also said that the devil's martyrs must earn hell so much harder than righteous martyrs earn heaven. Just look how whores, rascals, and murderers suffer so much more than any pious, quiet citizen or farmer.

172. But how do we present-day Christians want to keep this teaching on Christ's suffering now that secular lords have also become Christians? They do not tolerate stealing from or harming Christians, and their protection and shield should be not despised but gratefully used like all goods and creations of God. For any Christians under the rule of the Turks must hold such teachings in high regard and therefore suffer far more than we know or believe.

---

6 German: *barfüßer* (Latin: *discalceati*; literally, "without shoes"). A group of orders recognized by the Catholic Church that would not wear shoes. They based their tradition, for example, on Matt 10:10 or Mark 6:9.

7 Latin: *propter me, prophet iustitiam*. Luther paraphrased the German translation of the Bible reference for emphasis.

8 Latin: *non poena, sed causa facit martyrem*.

173. Among us today these most holy of all Christians, the papists, nowadays endure excessive torture of all kinds and carry a great cross. They can neither sleep nor rest because they find themselves incapable of sufficiently persecuting, murdering, and drowning the gospel and all who believe in it and filling the world with blood. And in this way, they allegedly honor God and sustain the holy church—for which they promise each other countless heavenly crowns of honor.

***

REVIEW QUESTIONS

1. In what ways do usurers resemble the devil?
2. Who is Cacus, and what is the special trick he employs to remain undetected?
3. What three things are pastors called to teach to the people?
4. In paragraph 171, Luther quotes Saint Augustine, saying, "Not the suffering but the right cause of suffering makes martyrs!" What does he mean by that? What contemporary examples of "false martyrs" come to mind?

STUDY QUESTIONS

1. Luther quotes Exodus 20:5 as a reference for the observation that "unjustly" acquired money never makes it into the third generation. Discuss this ancient observation. Do you know any confirming or contrary examples?
2. Luther quotes Saint Jerome, saying, "Every rich man is either unjust or heir to unjustly acquired property." In subsistence economies without growth—where just enough is produced to service all needs—this is certainly true: these are zero-sum constructs in which one party's gain can only be from another's loss. How is this different in economies that keep growing overall?

***

Part X

Where, Then, Is Our Suffering?

174. But jesting aside, where are we suffering in this way? We who enjoy the protection of the secular authorities, we who no one can take anything from or insult because even the authorities have accepted the word of God? Those other authorities who persecute the word of God cause their subjects enough suffering and affliction. We are seeing this and just said it above about the papists and their raving. Where then, I ask, is our suffering?

175. I will tell you right away: you only need to take one glance at all layers of society from bottom to top. There you find what you are looking for! You will find it in every pious Christian peasant who expresses Christian charity and faithfulness to his peasant neighbor or his poverty-stricken pastor—through giving, lending, counseling, and helping wherever there is need.

176. On the other hand, for every such Christian peasant, you will find more than a thousand unchristian peasants who do not give a penny—neither to pastor nor to neighbor—even letting them starve. Instead, they are stingy and grab and grub for themselves; they overprice, forge, fake and fleece, embezzle, seize, covertly steal, and rob wherever they can—be it from their employer, their pastor, or their neighbor. And if they just could draw the blood of everyone until they suck them dry—they would do that, too, to satisfy their avarice, which indeed can never be satisfied. All the pious and Christian peasants living in any principality will certainly fit into a single village—and not a large one at that. What about it?

177. I'd think these Christian peasants would teach you that you will have to observe the doctrine of suffering in order to overcome evil with patience. For the peasants in Israel behaved toward their priests, Levites, brothers, and friends the same way, as we read in Malachi [Mal 3:8].

178. The same thing you also see among the citizens. You will find such town halls where mayors and councilors seriously follow the gospel, or you will find that faithful and Christian citizen who happily gives, lends, helps, and so on. On the other hand, you will find lots of city halls and plenty more citizens who hate or despise the gospel.

179. As much as they can, they annoy, bedevil, and torment pastors and poor citizens alike, acting even stingier than any unchristian peasant. Moreover, they pursue veritable tyranny, power,[1] and honor toward the pastor, just as toward the poor man. So I think that you could probably gather all the pious, Christian councilmen and citizens of any principality in a single city that would likewise not have to be very large. Consider these Christian citizens master instructors, for they teach observing Christ's word of suffering.

180. After that, review nobility and officials, and count for me those who take God's word seriously! For above all others and out of great love, they are the ones who virtually gobble down the word of God. Whenever you find one who is serious about giving, lending, and helping his neighbor, you will again find more than one hundred of them who are doing the exact opposite and do so with great force. We certainly would not need an outsized castle to accommodate a principality's entire Christian, laudable, and pious nobility.

181. If, by the way, you still do not know the meaning of suffering according to the teachings of Christ, be so bold to try the following: where it contradicts them, cite God's word to one of these clodhoppers[2] or refuse to worship him as a god the way he likes to have it. There you will find what you are looking for!

182. We will render a particularly glorious and praiseworthy service to those people whose greed and usury we confront (in which they wholly drowned and sank lower than even the bottom of hell), whom we therefore consider non-Christians and to whom we neither give sacrament nor allow into the community of the church—our conscience would not allow it.

---

1 Instead of "power" in the sense of political power, the German term *Gewalt* could also be translated as "violence." Located in the context of the terms *tyranny* and *honor*, as above, translating it as "power" makes more sense.
2 See explanation of Luther's derogatory terms, p. 16.

183. Finally, take a look at our high nobility! To find one or two of them are Christian is as rare as venison in heaven![3] Meanwhile, the rest of them all remain in hell, together with the devil. As it is, they already inflict enough suffering and unhappiness among Christians.

CLERGY UNDER INTENSE ATTACK FROM THE DEVIL

184. Although the Lord has generally proclaimed and commanded such suffering to all of his Christians, he has especially commanded it to the apostles and their heirs in office. The devil is especially hostile to them because, by virtue of their office, they must publicly rebuke such vices. But that is exactly what they will not suffer, these peasants and citizens, noblemen, princes, and masters. Like their lord, the devil, they want to freely and with impunity do as they please. Then they additionally want to be honored and praised for it.

185. Therefore, the devil is hostile not only to pious pastors and preachers but also to wicked ones and to all scholars or, as he calls them, writers. For he fears any writer or scholar could one day become a preacher, and a wicked pastor might become a devout pastor later on. He finds this intolerable in his kingdom. This is no wonder, for if he had only laymen and no one learned, he knows how soon priests and books would perish. That is precisely why he is so hostile to all scholars and writers, even those who do not harm him but powerfully serve him. Who knows, he ought to be hostile even to all geese because of the quill pens the feathers of these birds provide.

186. That is why he now deploys this saying: "One ought not to let the priests become masters!" People do not talk like that out of concern that clergymen might actually become masters. You pastors yourself know best that pastors are strictly forbidden to become masters. Likewise, no one can deny this either: no pastor owns his parish; pastors are mere guests in their parish estates and must leave everything behind when they die.

187. Even if one or two of them actually succeed in buying a little house for their widows and orphans, all others remain nothing but veritable beggars. Therefore, they leave behind their widows and orphans, as beggars do. And if they really managed, with some effort, to acquire something of their own, down here they still have to live among lowly

---

3 That is to say, "very rarely."

peasants and citizens because, with ten gulden, they can neither ride high nor sit high.[4]

188. All this is known, seen, heard, and understood by the mockers; they understand it very well indeed. They nevertheless insult and ridicule such poor people, saying, "Priests shall never be masters!" This seems just like the rich man in the gospel who speaks of poor Lazarus [Luke 16:19–31], whom he refuses even the bread crusts and crumbs that fall for the dogs under his table: "Lazarus must not be master in my house!" Dear friend, just how much are these scorners like those who once crowned our Lord with thorns and then spit on him, saying, "Greetings, dear King"?

189. That is why I say people do not talk like that because they worry about the pastors becoming masters. They willfully invent such pretexts to muffle the ministry of preaching so that they can be all the freer and safer from hearing the truth about their punishable behavior.

190. The gospel needs such people or else it would soon perish; we need them if we are to suffer evil for Christ's sake. What the Lord says must hold true for our own people: "Truly I tell you, no prophet is accepted in the prophet's hometown" [Luke 4:24]. Christ also teaches, "It is impossible for a prophet to be killed outside of Jerusalem" [Luke 13:33]. And John says, "He came to what was his own, and his own people did not accept him" [John 1:11].[5]

191. If our gospel is the righteous light, then it must indeed shine in the darkness, but the darkness cannot understand it [John 1:5]. If then we do not like this and long to have a different world, then we must either go out into the world or else create a different world that does what we want or what God wants [1 Cor 5:10]. This world in which we live does not and will not do it. We should accept this and happily surrender into it.

192. We do not read that one of the old prophets was strangled by neighboring heathen or enemies, but rather, the people of God and its kings persecuted them to the ends of the earth like Ahab persecuted Elijah [1 Kgs 19:14]. And in Jerusalem—that holy city of God, the bridal chamber of Christ, the dearest fruit on earth, the joyful hostess of all angels, and the housemother of all the saints—even this Jerusalem had to murder God's prophets and ultimately crucify even the Lord himself [Matt 23:27]. Likewise, the church could not be eliminated by the world's power and skillfulness, not even that of the Roman Empire, which was

---

4 That is to say, "attain high societal ranks."
5 Evidently, Luther uses irony here to make his point.

the most powerful and rampantly raging against it. But then the holy fathers, bishops, and teachers went after it with heresy first, then with violence, until finally that most holy father himself[6] became church, God, and everything in one. Thus, Christ was indeed crucified and buried together with all the prophets, apostles, and saints.

193. Therefore, it is the duty of our preachers, pastors, and indeed all Christians to do justice and honor to our gospel: first by preaching false doctrine and second by reverting to violence. This is especially because both—namely, lies and murder—were the devil's arms from the beginning [John 8:44]. God knows, our agitators[7] gave a head start to the lies. Peasants and citizens, nobles and gentlemen confidently helped them with ingratitude, contempt, hatred, pride, and other deceit. But with this fine prelude already started, the main song will soon begin—if it is not already half-sung and performed anyway.

* * *

Review Questions

1. Where can we actually find genuine suffering for Christ?
2. Why does the devil especially attack pastors and clergy?
3. Why should the devil be hostile to geese?
4. In paragraph 191, Luther recommends we accept our present world as it is. What does he mean?

Study Questions

1. According to a 2020 survey, almost nine out of ten members of the 117th Congress assess themselves to be Christian—468 out of 531.[8] At least nine out of any ten of the US's highest politicians are, in their own view, "God's servants"—very different from what Luther

---

6 That is, the pope.

7 German: *rottengeister*. See also footnote 5, Part IX.

8 In the House and Senate, 88 percent are Christian, and about 62 percent of those are Protestant. The numbers are roughly the same as in previous Congresses. See "Faith on the Hill—the Religious Composition of the 117th Congress," *Pew Research Center's Religion & Public Life Project* (blog), January 4, 2021, https://www.pewforum.org/2021/01/04/faith-on-the-hill-2021/.

told us (paragraph 183). Why do you think the numbers are this way? Are there reasons to doubt the delegates' self-assessments?

2. US Congresses have been overwhelmingly Christian for many decades, regardless of what party is in power. Discuss how you think they are doing on Luther's account: What are they doing well, what could be done better, and where do they fail, according to Luther's yardstick (paragraphs 178 through 180)?

3. Find out how Christians are represented in the leadership of your municipality. How are they measuring up to Luther's account?

* * *

Part XI

Our Sacred Duty

194. But if you risk your life and confidently call them unchristian, call them enemies of God who despise his Word, they will tolerate it much less than Jerusalem would tolerate it, the holy city that was called a whorehouse and murder pit by Isaiah [Isa 56:7;[1] Jer 7:11]. The same is true of most of our Christians today. Although they want to be evangelicals[2] and seemingly keep high the Word and behave like proper saints, at the same time, they fight those pastors and preachers who actually preach the Word and tell them the truth. Jerusalem also kept the word of God high, yet the prophets should not preach it. If they did anyway, they had to die and perish.

195. But what would we preachers, pastors, and scribes complain about? Just look at the world itself, and observe how everyone "serves" their peers with Christian love and faithfulness! Observe how one country hates the other—as Italians, Spaniards, Hungarians, and Germans— how one prince treats the other, how one gentleman, citizen, peasant "serves" another: by envying, hating, hacking, dominating, harming, and inflicting every conceivable misfortune on him or, at the very least, wishing such things upon him!

196. See also how everyone would like to have everything for themselves and for themselves to be the only one! Looking at such conduct

---

1 Luther quotes Isa 3:14–17. Besides Jer 7:11, WA also gives Isa 56:7 in the side notes. More likely seems Isa 1:21: "How the faithful city has become a whore! She that was full of justice, righteousness lodged in her—but now murderers!"

2 Luther uses *evangelisch sein*. This could be translated also as "to be Protestant." At any rate, *evangelisch sein* has no overlap in meaning with the American use of the term *evangelical* as a variant of Christian tradition and lacks all its connotations.

with our evangelical hearts, we must conclude that it is not people but indeed hordes of veritable devils that rampage around in human masks. One wonders how the world lasts even for a single year.

GOD'S POWER AND WISDOM AID YOU

197. Where only can we find the power that—despite such disunity and enmity; despite such hatred and envy, the robbing, stealing, scratching, tearing, damaging; and despite all this unspeakable malice—can save the world and prevent it from going to ruin every day anew? It is God's wonderful and almighty power and wisdom we have to feel and grasp in all this. Otherwise, this situation could not last for so long.

198. Therefore, do not worry where you will find suffering! There is plenty to go around. Be a good Christian, preacher, pastor, citizen, peasant, nobleman, and lord. Do your duty diligently and faithfully! Let the devil worry where to find a branch and make it into a cross for you, and let the world worry where to find a ripcord to make into a whip for your skin, even though the authorities mean well for you. For no authority will be so clever and powerful as to be able to shield and protect you from the devil, from evil people, and from all ill—even if they were especially pious and diligent.

199. Therefore, just be a true Christian who suffers for the sake of God with an unassuming heart, and do not self-invent causes for your suffering as do the false, fervent martyrs and monks or the useful rascals who bring misfortune or the gallows upon themselves by their wickedness!

200. Just think about Aesop's chicken,[3] which was bitten by the roosters! Observing that the roosters bit one another, it consoled itself, saying, "I now will better like enduring my sufferings because I see that they likewise bite each other." Should the world not bite us Christians just as she bites and kicks herself so shamefully? Why, then, do we want to have it better in the world than the world has for herself, since she must endure herself more than she can stand?

201. May this suffice about the law and doctrine of Christ on how to donate, lend, and suffer, ensuring there is no room left for usury and avarice among Christians. Should usury and avarice still spread, those who do it are certainly not Christians—despite all their boasting and whatever they claim. For Christ says in Matthew, "No man can serve two

---

3 Luther references Aesop's fable "The Gamecocks and the Partridge."

masters. . . . Ye cannot serve God and mammon" [Matt 6:24 KJV].⁴ And
Saint Paul declares, "Idolaters . . . the greedy . . . none of these will inherit
the kingdom of God" [1 Cor 6:9–10]. Here, he calls stinginess "idolatry,"
as by now, thank God, everyone knows.

Can Usurers Hope to Reach Salvation?

202. But if Mammon's servant—who is nothing but a miser and whose
life is pure idolatry—cannot reach salvation, where does this leave the
usurer? Whose servant should we call him, when we already call any miser
the "devil's servant"? After all, a miser and a usurer are not the same.

203. A miser can be stingy with his own goods—and yet never takes
anything away from anyone else, strangles no one, and murders no one
by his own hand or doing. Rather, such a man does only like the rich man
in the Gospel did insofar as he does not help where he ought to [Luke
16:19]. In this way, he causes death and harm only by watching how it
happens, though he could and should prevent it, as the well-known saying of Saint Ambrose testifies: "Feed the hungry. For if you do not feed
him, it is as if you strangled him."⁵

204. A usurer, on the other hand, is an active murderer. Not only
does he not help the hungry man; he also rips away from his mouth
that morsel of bread that God and pious people have donated to him
to maintain his body. A usurer does not care if the entire world dies of
hunger—if only he can have his profit.⁶

A Popular Interjection

205. "Yes," you say, "I am not stingy and do not overpower any poor man
but only the rich; that is, only those who have it; that is why I do not kill
and destroy anyone." I thank you, my dear rascal, for your statement. First
of all, for the fact that you at least self-confess to be a scrooge and a usurer;
that is, you are the devil's servant and an enemy of God and of all people.
And second, for teaching us how you do not destroy and murder the poor

---

4 Contemporary translations often use the words *wealth* or *money* in place of *Mammon*. Luther uses *Mammon* throughout his text to indicate the idolatrous nature
   of an outright worship of money and wealth.

5 Latin: *pasce esurientem, si non pavisti, occidisti.*

6 Luther wrote "Wucher," which translates literally to *usury*.

but "only" suck dry the rich and well-off and thus also self-confess to be a thief and robber! That is truly well done and well-apologized because I did not know that before! By all means, you should continue to try charming me into believing I was wrong when I scolded you as a big murderer and robber and therefore I ought to revoke my scolding. But first, listen to my answer, you smart-alecky usurer and murderer!

206. After all, about whom is most of your usury? Isn't it exclusively about the poor? Are not they the ones who, because of your usury, can retain neither a penny nor a bite of bread? Take Nehemiah, for example: About whom was that usury described there, where, in the end, the poor people took their houses, farms, vineyards, fields, and everything they had—even their children—and sold them to the usurer [Neh 5:3]? Likewise, ask who was going to Rome, Athens, and other cities where, as has already been said, citizens became slaves as a result of usury? Was not that about the poor there too? Yes, all these people were rich once, but usury devoured them all, including their very own bodies.

207. May the devil thank you for not abusing the poor by usury. Just tell me, what usurious gain did you expect from those who have nothing to begin with? We know quite well that you do not exercise your usury on empty wallets but start with the rich and turn them into beggars. And does it not just follow from your beautiful apology that your usury rips nothing from the poor, that you do indeed murder among the rich people? You make them beggars and drive them into poverty, even though you were meant to help them out of poverty. So with this pretty excuse, you're not just the killer of the poor but also the killer of the rich—indeed, exclusively the rich. And you are such a formidable god in the world that you make poor and rich into the same thing. You do not murder them until you first make them poor—that is your great love and friendship!

208. Moreover, even though the rich can endure the price inflation caused by your usury, the poor man cannot. He often does not even have a single gulden per week to buy food, and he also has many children. Therefore, he cannot even buy enough bread with his hard work because your close-fistedness and usury increase prices and make everything more expensive. In this case, then, who is actually the subject of your usury?

209. Dear friend, just go ahead and apologize again, saying you only make things more expensive and practice usury so the rich have cause to give to the poor that much more in alms and, in this way, can earn the kingdom of heaven. Indeed, you subject the rich to your usury in two

ways: one directly, the other by means of those poor people they have to donate to so that, in the end, you will gain everything even sooner. All that is missing now is your self-praise for having done a good work while also serving the rich by giving them increased opportunities to do good works. In what other way could you possibly achieve an even better reputation, one even more suitable of a usurer? For in the exact same way, the devil himself unceasingly gives us reasons to do good works: because he wracks many people who then are obliged to help for the sake of God.

Usurers Will Go to Hell—but without Their Pastors

210. In a short time, your usury and stinginess have made it so that someone who was able to feed themselves on one hundred gulden a few years ago now cannot even feed themselves with two hundred gulden. The usurers sit far away in Leipzig, Augsburg, and Frankfurt and in like cities seemingly just trading with money. Nonetheless, we feel them here on our food market and in our kitchen because we can keep neither cent nor dime. We pastors and preachers, together with those who own no business and live off interest payments—that is, all those who cannot increase their incomes—feel quite unmistakably how closely the usurers breathe down our necks. Next to us, they eat from our kitchens, they drink most of what is in our cellars, they press and scrape from us so that our bodies and lives hurt. Farmers, citizens, and nobles can at least increase the price of their grain and their labor, doubling their income or tripling it. They therefore can endure usury more easily. But those who have to burn through their savings have no choice but to endure maltreatment and let themselves be choked.

211. Yet preaching no longer helps, for their usuring made them numb, blind, and senseless; usurers therefore do not hear, see, or feel anything anymore. But we preachers have to make sure that we are acquitted on their last day, when they have to go to hell. By then, they should have no excuse, should not be able to blame us, their pastors, because we failed to properly admonish, punish, and instruct them. We should not be obliged to go to hell with them on account of their sins! No, they should go to hell all by themselves! For by then, we have done our part; with great diligence, we punished and instructed them in accordance with our office. Their blood and sins shall be and remain on their heads alone; it shall not come to us!

* * *

Review Questions

1. In paragraph 206, Luther writes that usury consumed all the possessions of those once rich, "including their very own bodies." What does he mean by this phrase?

2. Luther responds to the common excuse of usurers, who say they only take from the rich. In Luther's final analysis, who is most affected by usury?

3. What is a major motivation for pastors to admonish and punish the known usurers in their congregations?

Study Questions

1. In paragraph 203, Luther quotes Saint Ambrose, saying, "Feed the hungry. For if you do not feed him, it is as if you strangled him." Would you agree that today, this could also be said for basic health care, perhaps in the sense of "Treat the sick. For if you do not treat him where there is a cure, it is as if you injured or murdered him through negligence?" How would death from lack of access to basic health care be different from death by starvation from lack of access to food? Why do you agree or disagree?

2. As Nobel Prize–winning economist Amartya Sen observed forty years ago, famines are no longer happening because there is not enough food. Instead, people are made to starve because they cannot pay for the food they need to live.[7] Discuss Sen's insight and whether Luther would agree or not.

3. To what popular modern economic argument do Luther's words point in paragraph 209? How does this resonate with you? Why?

4. At the beginning of paragraph 209, Luther repeats one of his key criticisms of the Catholic doctrine of his times. What is he referring to?

* * *

---

7 Amartya Sen, *Poverty and Famines: An Essay on Entitlement and Deprivation* (Oxford: Clarendon, 1981), https://www.prismaweb.org/nl/wp-content/uploads/2017/06/Poverty-and-famines%E2%94%82Amartya-Sen%E2%94%821981.pdf.

Part XII

Parting Advice

212. Finally, so that the misers and usurers do not think we want to do away with their craft or ruin it altogether, we would like to give them a good and faithful piece of advice so that they get to fully—indeed, overabundantly—exercise miserliness and usury. Because you preachers can name a rich Lord who likes providing gains to his usurers, go seek and invite misers and usurers from wherever they come so they can exercise with your Lord their miserliness and usury as much and as high as they can! He will pay them plenty in usury, not just 10 or 20 percent, but 100 percent interest for one gulden, even a thousand for one hundred! This Lord has so many silver and gold mountains that he can do it easily and do it well.

213. This Lord is called God, the Creator of heaven and earth. In the gospel, through his Son, God leaves us this offer: give and borrow, and it shall be given to you again not only the same but much more—namely, a full measure, a measure shaken, a jam-packed measure, an overflowing measure [Luke 6:38]! So bring now your sack and wallet, barrel and barn, you hear? It shall be returned to you so much that all sacks and barrels are too few and too small, and they become so full that nothing more can fit in them, and they instead must overflow. And again, "Everyone who has left houses or brothers or sisters or father or mother or children or fields, for my name's sake, will receive a hundredfold, and will inherit eternal life" [Matt 19:29].

214. Why not exercise stinginess and usury here, where greed is satiable, and the urge for excessive gain can be quenched? Why pursue insatiable avarice and usury among your neighbors, who can only give back little and therefore cannot satiate your avarice but instead infuriate it and make it thirstier? Is it not the wretched devil, who prevents one from

misering and usuring much of anything from this rich Lord—this rich Lord who offers to anyone to become his debtor, interest payer, and liege and pay usurious interest rates where no one else will? He himself calls it usury and wants such usurers. In the Proverbs of Solomon, it is said, "Whoever donates to and is kind to the poor practices usury with the Lord"[1] [Prov 19:17].

215. So where are you stingy, insatiable usurers? Come here and usuriously obtain life and all bliss—here temporarily and there forever—and all the time without any harm to your neighbor. Come here, all who by your accursed usury become murderers and rogues to fellow men, who are turned into the absolute worst and most despised people on earth. Come here, all whose usury makes them lose body and soul forever—and yet, as already said above, they are capable neither of keeping their riches nor of bequeathing them to the third heir! Here you can be proper and holy usurers, usurers who are dear to God, all angels, and people alike and who also, in this way, can never lose their usurious reward.

216. Consider now, are not human beings nonsensical and possessed of all the devils, since they despise such a rich Lord, with his gorgeous and eternal invitation to practice usury with him, and instead turn to the damaging, damned, murderous, and thieving usury that itself cannot stay and only pushes them to hell?

PASTORS: LET GO OF THE USURERS

217. Therefore, a usurer and a miser is truly not a rightful person; he also does not actually sin the human way! He must be a werewolf, worse still than any tyrant, murderer, and robber, as evil as the devil himself! For he sits not as an enemy but as a friend and fellow citizen in the protection and peace of the community—and still robs and murders more horribly than any enemy, murderer, and arsonist. Therefore, if one ravages and beheads robbers, murderers, and raiders, how much more should one first break on the wheel and torture all usurers, chase away all penny-pinchers, curse and behead especially those who ruthlessly cause price inflation, as nobles and peasants do today and indeed do so most eagerly!

---

1 The author's translation of the actual text Luther used in this tract when he quotes this Bible verse. Today's NRSV version of Prov 19:17 reads, "Whoever is kind to the poor lends to the Lord, and will be repaid in full."

218. Let me tell you: let go of them! See to it, pastor, that you do not participate in their sins, as stated above! Let them die like dogs! Let them be completely devoured by the devil, body and soul! Exclude them from the sacrament, do not baptize them, and do not let them participate in Christian community! Because there will be a plague about Germany that cannot stay away for much longer. And then, stinginess and usury will be chiefs of the deadly sins for which we will all suffer God's wrath and torment because we have tolerated such damned people among us and neither punished nor disciplined them but instead kept fellowship with them.

219. But especially the princes and lords will have to answer for the fact that they wield their swords in vain and enable such murderers and robbers (usurers and misers) to kill and rob unhindered in their lands through usury and wanton inflation! Even if they should go unpunished for their own sins, God will punish them for the sins of these evildoers so they will impoverish and perish, lose land and people, or he will let their dynasty and tribe wither and dry up—as already has happened to so many of them!

220. God opposes usury and greed, yet no one realizes this because it is not simple murder and robbery. Rather, usury is a more diverse, insatiable murder and robbery. Thus everyone should see to his worldly and spiritual office as commanded to punish the wicked and protect the pious.

CONCLUSION

221. Let this be enough for explaining usury! A preacher may well learn much more from the books that were written at all times against usury and stinginess. Then he can preach about all the horrible and terrible examples to show how God—and even the devil—always dealt with usurers and avaricious people. How he shamefully murdered their bodies and their souls and terminated their tribes to the last person; how he allowed their goods and belongings to be completely destroyed. At that time, no one believed that God's wrath could be so strong about them— just as few as our modern usurers believe it. But then they experienced it as will those who we see daily today and who will continue to offer us more such examples in the future.

222. I am not referring to *Zinskauf* here because a right and honest purchase is not usury. Thank God we know very well what a *Zinskauf*

is by secular law—namely, that identified collateral should be there and also that not too much interest shall be taken.[2] But this wasn't our topic here, and therefore, let everyone make sure that it is a fair and honest purchase for them! If, as we currently observe, the *Zinskauf* is again abused so strongly and astonishingly across all trades—perhaps this time, someone else may explain this in detail, for I did that already some fifteen years ago.

223. God be gracious to us and make us pious that we honor his name, increase his kingdom, and do his will! AMEN.

* * *

REVIEW QUESTIONS

1. In paragraph 213, Luther refers to a "measure shaken." What does he mean by that?

2. In paragraph 222, Luther refers to *Zinskauf*. What is it, and why is it not usury when done right?

STUDY QUESTIONS

1. In paragraphs 212 through 215, Luther reaches out to all those who find themselves usurers but want to change their ways. Discuss his pastoral proposal: Did you expect him to extend such an olive branch? Why or why not?

2. Historically, many claimed Martin Luther to be socially conservative. His "Two Kingdoms" theology, they say, promoted both subservience to divinely willed authorities and ethical quietism. Indeed, many congregations today cannot bring themselves to speak up on social issues at all, claiming that their Lutheran delineation would conflict with it. After reading Luther's "Exhortation," what do you think?

3. What, if anything, in Luther's "Exhortation" speaks most directly to economics in today's world?

---

2 See more on this in the section *Zinskauf,* p. 17.

Leader's Notes

Part I

Review Question 1: See paragraph 3.

Review Question 2: This is an example of "lending": nothing except for the original good in its original condition is returned.

Review Question 3: Luther would find your son's action usurious: The additional gas in the tank is a payment of kinds. This activity would remain simple lending if you replaced only the gas you used up. Your son asking more in return turns this transaction into usury. If he did not ask for it, and you filled his car's tank out of your own impulse, that extra gas would be a gift to your son, freely made and happily given.

Review Question 4: See paragraphs 7, 10, 14, and 18.

Study Question 3: Paragraph 18 provides Luther's view.

Part II

Review Question 1: See paragraph 27.

Review Question 2: See page 18.

Study Question 1: In some denominations, it is customary that pastors, in parallel with their theological education, obtain a degree in some nontheological field. For example, in some countries, it is common for Catholic clergy to have a degree in economics.

Study Question 2: For a summary of common practices, see Thomas Oliphant, "A GOP Fleecing of Card Users," *Boston Sunday Globe*, August 29, 2004, http://archive.boston.com/news/globe/editorial _opinion/oped/articles/2004/08/29/a_gop_fleecing_of_card_users/. Oliphant, a Pulitzer Prize winner, suggests the private finance industry should be called "usury business." Among other industry practices, Oliphant explains "universal default": "You miss a payment on some other bill (it could be a $50 phone bill) and all of a sudden your credit card interest rate soars to anywhere from 30 percent to as much as 48 percent." This practice is a textbook example of usurious lending through hypothetical damage: just because the phone bill went unpaid, no damage on other loans has actually occurred.

Study Question 3: The low cost of their own borrowing and low inflation do not change the argument for hypothetical damage. If anything, bank profits are increased because the Fed keeps their costs low. Not passing on this advantage could be interpreted as aggravating the case for usury.

Part III

Review Question 1: See paragraph 48.

Review Question 2: See paragraph 50.

Study Question 1: A discussion starter could be the popular quest to uncover the way to pay the absolute minimum of taxes one owes—privately and in commerce. In large corporations, it is often profitable to pay entire departments of lawyers to interpret tax law in ways that minimize payments, mostly in legal but occasionally in not-so-legal ways. Looking at the political landscape, every year, the United States has a few companies that pay zero dollars in taxes, and many more pay token amounts on nevertheless sizable profits. You could discuss, for example, how it can at all be possible for a company like shoe manufacturer Nike to pay zero dollars of federal income tax on almost $2.9 billion of US pretax income in 2020 and instead enjoy a tax rebate of $109 million. See Matthew Gardner and Steve Wamhoff, "55 Corporations Paid $0 in Federal Taxes on 2020 Profits," Institute on Taxation and Economic Policy, April 2021, https://itep.sfo2.digitaloceanspaces .com/040221-55-Profitable-Corporations-Zero-Corporate-Taxes.pdf.

Study Question 2: You could begin finding out how many cable companies or electric power companies offer services in your town. Many places have just one offering—a monopoly inviting uncompetitive pricing. One example for another recent cartel was documented in 2000, involving four companies selling vitamins (Department of Justice, "Four Foreign Executives of Leading European Vitamin Firms Agree to Plead Guilty to Participating in International Vitamin Cartel," April 6, 2000, https://www.justice.gov/archive/atr/public/ press_releases/2000/4494.htm). Examples of elevated prices due to an oligopoly or a monopoly (for example, through a patent) can be observed in pharmaceuticals. One US example is the offering of insulin by just four companies at prices some ten times what they cost in Canada. See Michael Sainato, "'Medication or Housing': Why Soaring Insulin Prices Are Killing Americans," *The Guardian*, September 23, 2019, https://www.theguardian.com/society/2019/sep/23/diabetes-americans-soaring-insulin-prices. In his book, economist Thomas Philippon makes the case that most of America's economy has abandoned competitive price formation. This forces consumers to pay elevated prices on goods and services. See Thomas Philippon, *The Great Reversal: How America Gave Up on Free Markets* (Cambridge, MA: Belknap Press of Harvard University Press, 2019).

Part IV

Review Question 1: See page 16 for the explanation of the term.

Review Question 2: See paragraph 69.

Study Question 1: Many states have legislation against what is also known as "predatory lending." Actual legislation varies by state, since firms are incorporated and often bound by laws of the state they incorporate in. Regulatory arbitrage opportunities, especially in the states of Delaware and South Carolina, seem to have rendered much modern usury legislation ineffective. See, for example, Will Kenton, "Usury Laws," Investopedia, July 18, 2022, https://www.investopedia.com/terms/u/usury-laws.asp.

Study Question 5: Indeed, late in 2021, the news agency Associated Press reported Afghani people selling their kids to be able to pay for food. See Associated Press, "Parents Selling Children Shows Desperation in Afghanistan," reported on National Public Radio, December 31, 2021, https://www.npr.org/2021/12/31/1069428211/parents-selling-children-shows-desperation-in-afghanistan.

Part V

Review Question 1: See paragraphs 81 and 82.

Review Question 3: See paragraphs 87 and 88.

Study Question 1: Luther considered any trade practice taking advantage of the neighbor a violation of the seventh commandment. This includes but is not at all limited to usury as explained in the introduction (see "Sin of Usury Not Limited to Monetary Interest," p. 4).

Luther also explained this view in his 1520 treatise *On Good Works* (LW 44:15–114).

Study Question 2: Investment credit typically creates new means of production, such as machines or factories. In this sense, any interest on such credits is a share of the profits that both parties expect from the investment. These profits will pay interest and repay the principal. By contrast, consumer credits typically do not create or enable new means of production; they are spent buying goods that are then readily consumed. Therefore, there is no future profit with which both parties could hope to cover interest and repayment.

Study Question 3: Luther's argument would not apply to business loans, especially not to loans given to limited liability companies. For even if the loan turns sour and the firm goes under, the liability limitation legally protects its owners from personal ruin. For example, common shareholders are typically not liable for a corporation's debt: they may lose their shares, but their liability stops there.

Study Question 4: The case for an unconscionable clause or contract requires proof that one party would be surprised or unduly disadvantaged by it. However, in the United States, taking on economic risk because of an inferior negotiation position is not typically considered "unconscionable." As an example, *federal* student loans are typically forgiven if the borrower (student) dies. However, there is no law requiring commercial lenders to cancel *private* student loans upon the death of the borrower. Only about half of private student loan programs offer death discharges similar to the discharges on federal student loans. You could discuss the merits of a hypothetical case of an unconscionable clause for private contracts not providing a death discharge.

Study Question 5: Luther mentions one exemption in paragraphs 85 through 87.

Part VI

Review Question 1: See paragraphs 85 through 87. Usurers must be treated this way because a usurer is "an idol worshipper who is unbelieving because he serves Mammon. He therefore cannot have or receive forgiveness of sins, and he can have or receive neither the grace of Christ nor the communion of saints" (paragraph 87).

Review Question 2: See paragraph 104 and on.

Study Question 1: See paragraph 109.

Study Question 3: A complex topic, so tread carefully here. Keep in mind that Luther's time does not distinguish between credit for personal consumption and credit for business investments. As a discussion starter, consider Warren Buffett's behavior. He bought his home for $31,500 back in 1958. In 2003, it was assessed to be worth around $700,000. He's still living in it: Nathaniel Lee, "Warren Buffett Lives in a Modest House That's Worth .001% of His Total Wealth," Business Insider, November 10, 2020, https://www.businessinsider.com/warren-buffett-modest-home-bought-31500-looks-2017-6?op=1. As of summer 2020, the billionaire investor has donated $37 billion worth of Berkshire Hathaway stock to various charities: Michael J. de la Merced, "Warren Buffett Gives Another $2.9 Billion to Charity," *New York Times*, July 8, 2020, https://www.nytimes.com/2020/07/08/business/dealbook/warren-buffett-donations.html.

Study Question 6: For US tax revenue information, see the data of the Congressional Budget Office ("An Update to the Budget and Economic Outlook: 2017 to 2027," June 29, 2017, https://www.cbo.gov/publication/52801) and links therein.

Part VII

Review Question 1: See paragraphs 111 through 113.

Review Question 2: The cubit is an ancient unit of length that may have originated in Egypt close to five thousand years ago. It spans about eighteen inches. Luther uses this image saying that the standard of the Bible judging our actions stands firm and will not vary: just as we do not change the unit of length because a different piece of cloth is measured.

Review Question 3: He is referring to indulgences as sold by the medieval Catholic Church. The merit held for sale was supposedly supplied out of the abundance of merits accumulated by the saints, made available widely across Europe in exchange for money by the medieval Catholic organization.

Review Question 4: He says the Catholic Church claims Luther's teaching on good works as their own while attributing their own teachings to Luther. See paragraphs 116 through 118.

Review Question 6: See paragraph 127 and especially 130.

Study Question 1: Practical consequences would include constant confusion about what to expect from one another: When I deal with you, are you "perfect" or rather of the laxer kind? Will your behavior change on me?

Study Question 2: A common view is that social welfare is unaffordably expensive. To discuss affordability further, you might consider the Supplemental Nutrition Assistance Program (SNAP, formerly the Food Stamp Program). For instance, it supplied benefits to about 40 million Americans in 2018 at a cost of $57.1 billion. "Government Social Benefits: To Persons: Federal: Supplemental Nutrition Assistance Program (SNAP)," *FRED, Federal Reserve Bank of St. Louis*, August 6, 2021, https://fred.stlouisfed.org/series/TRP6001A027NBEA. For comparison, see budget amounts for selected US departments (https://www.usaspending.gov/agency): Department of Defense, $991 billion; Department of Agriculture, $317 billion; Federal Deposit Insurance Corporation, $121 billion; Department of Labor, $84 billion; Department of State, $59 billion; and the Environmental Protection Agency, $28 billion. The entire federal budget is around $8.325 trillion.

Part VIII

Review Question 1: See paragraphs 134 and 136.

Review Question 2: This is leading to violating the first commandment. For more on that, see paragraph 141 and on.

Review Question 3: See paragraph 140.

Review Question 4: It is yet another instance of attempting to buy salvation through our own work and effort. See paragraph 143.

Review Question 6: See paragraph 152.

Study Question 1: See paragraph 135. Also keep in mind that there are usually substantial tax benefits to the donor for such charitable giving.

Part IX

Review Question 1: See paragraph 158.

Review Question 2: See paragraphs 164 and 165.

Review Question 3: See paragraphs 162 and 166.

Study Question 1: Interestingly, a recent study shows 90 percent of family fortunes are indeed depleted by the third generation. See Rhymer Rigby, "Disinheriting Your Children Might Be for Their Own Good," *Financial Times*, October 15, 2019, https://www.ft.com/content/eb4a390a-d926-11e9-9c26-419d783e10e8.

Study Question 2: In economies that grow and where the growth is shared across all strata of life, it is genuinely possible that one party makes a fortune without taking it away from anyone. In such economies, Saint Jerome's saying needs to be applied with great care. For example, it would be tough to argue that those who became rich owning Microsoft or Apple shares made their fortune at the expense of their fellow beings. Growth and fortune resulting from genuine innovation do not work like fortune building in the stagnant, zero-sum economies that were the only kind Saint Jerome could experience.

Part X

Review Question 1: See paragraphs 175 and 181. On the rarity of such suffering, see the paragraphs that follow through 183.

Review Question 2: See paragraph 184.

Review Question 3: See the end of paragraph 185. An example of Luther's frequent use of irony.

Review Question 4: See paragraphs 191 and 192.

Part XI

Review Question 1: He means that in the end, just to survive, they sold themselves into slavery after they were deprived of all other means.

Review Question 2: See paragraph 208. The usury to the rich knocks through to the poor because prices rise for everyone. Many on fixed incomes also lack ways to adjust their remuneration as the cost of living increases.

Review Question 3: See paragraph 211.

Study Question 1: The United States is the sole exception in the Western canon of developed countries that does not afford its citizens universal health care. Instead, health care is contingent on gainful employment—if your employer extends this benefit. As a consequence, a 2016 CDC study finds that among America's poor or nearly poor, roughly one in four people lack access to health care (see Michael E. Martinez and Brian W. Ward, "Health Care Access and Utilization Among Adults Aged 18–64, by Poverty Level: United States, 2013–2015," NCHS Data Brief No. 262, October 2016, https://www.cdc.gov/nchs/products/databriefs/db262.htm). The rest of developed countries have implemented health care aligned with the idea that basic health care is a human right on par with the right to proper food.

Study Question 2: In Luther's times, bad harvests, sometimes occurring in consecutive years and over extended regions, were unavoidable. Long-distance trade in today's sense was emerging, but not for staple foods. In that sense, while Sen's insight is valid for today's world, it cannot be blindly applied to Luther's times. What remains true, as explained in the introduction, is that even in Luther's Wittenberg, some famines were manufactured or at least aggravated by food speculators cornering the market for better prices. For such situations, as we read in paragraph 204, for example, Luther would indeed agree with Sen's insight.

Study Question 3: In modern times, asymmetrical tax cuts favoring "the rich" more than groups with lower incomes are typically justified by arguing that these savings on taxes provide more funds to invest in and create jobs. Luther might have thought of something similar when he wrote, "All that is missing now is your self-praise for having done a good work while also serving the rich by giving them increased opportunities to do good works." Known today as "trickle-down economics," economist John Kenneth Galbraith famously ridiculed this thoroughly discredited idea as "horse and sparrow" theory: "If you feed the horse enough oats, some will pass through to the road for the sparrows" (John Kenneth Galbraith, "Recession Economics," *New York Review*, accessed May 19, 2022, https://www.nybooks.com/articles/1982/02/04/recession-economics/).

Study Question 4: It is the medieval Catholic teaching that God created the poor so the righteous could pay their way to salvation through almsgiving. See, for example, Lindberg, *Beyond Charity*.

Part XII

Review Question 1: Most piles of granular material in a container filled to the fullest—think of rice, grain, or beans—will settle when shaken or vibrated. So a shaken-down measure refilled to the fullest will contain more grains per volume than after it was originally poured. Every farmer and citizen would have been familiar with this experience from daily practice, and Luther uses this idea to explain how filled-to-the-brim God's measures of return will be.

Study Question 2: Many theologians wholeheartedly disagree with those claiming a socially silent and politically docile Luther. Prominently among them is Carter Lindberg, whose book *Beyond Charity: Reformation Initiatives for the Poor* contains a fulminant refutation of such claims. The idea of Luther as a social quietist simply does not hold up to the evidence. The "Exhortation" you just read is but one example. Throughout his life, Luther's faith drove him to continually speak out for the socially and economically disadvantaged of his time, and he urged political leaders to enact measures to mitigate their hardships. The Further Reading at the end of this book includes the *Forgotten Luther* series and other publications that further elaborate on this topic.

Further Reading

Braaten, Conrad A., and Ryan P. Cumming, eds. *The Forgotten Luther III: Reclaiming a Vision of Global Community*. Minneapolis: Fortress, 2021.

Cumming, Ryan P., ed. *The Forgotten Luther II: Reclaiming the Church's Public Witness*. Minneapolis: Fortress, 2019.

Kolb, Robert, and Timothy J. Wengert, eds. *The Book of Concord*. Minneapolis: Fortress, 2000.

Lindberg, Carter. *Beyond Charity: Reformation Initiatives for the Poor*. Minneapolis: Fortress, 1993.

———. "Luther on a Market Economy." *Lutheran Quarterly* 30 (2016): 373–392.

Lindberg, Carter, and Paul Wee, eds. *The Forgotten Luther: Reclaiming the Social-Economic Dimension of the Reformation*. Minneapolis: Lutheran University Press; Fortress, 2016.

Luther, Martin. *D. Martin Luthers Werke: Kritische Gesamtausgabe*. Edited by J. K. F. Knaake. 69 vols. Weimar: H. Böhlau, 1883–1929.

———. *Luther's Works*. Edited by Helmut T. Lehmann, Jaroslav Pelikan, Christopher Boyd Brown, and Benjamin T. G. Mayes. American ed. Saint Louis: Concordia (vols. 1–30); Philadelphia: Fortress (vols. 31–55), 1955–1986.

Rieth, Ricardo. "Luther on Greed." *Lutheran Quarterly* 15 (2001): 336–351. Reprinted in *Harvesting Martin Luther's Reflections on Theology, Ethics, and the Church*, edited by Timothy J. Wengert, 152–168. Grand Rapids, MI: Eerdmans, 2004.

———. "Luther's Treatment of Economic Life." In *The Oxford Handbook of Martin Luther's Theology*, edited by Robert Kolb, Irene Dingel, and L'ubomír Batka, 383–396. Oxford: Oxford University Press, 2014.

Sandel, Michael J. *What Money Can't Buy: The Moral Limits of Markets*. Reprint ed. New York: Farrar, Straus and Giroux, 2013.

Tanner, Kathryn. *Christianity and the New Spirit of Capitalism*. New Haven, CT: Yale University Press, 2019.

————. *The Politics of God: Christian Theologies and Social Justice*. Minneapolis: Fortress, 1992.

Torvend, Samuel. *Luther and the Hungry Poor: Gathered Fragments*. Minneapolis: Fortress, 2008.